Facilitating Communication For Business

NATIONAL BUSINESS EDUCATION YEARBOOK, NO. 26

Editor: JAMES CALVERT SCOTT
        Utah State University
        Logan, Utah

Published by:

National Business Education Association
1914 Association Drive
Reston, Virginia 22091

FACILITATING COMMUNICATION FOR BUSINESS

Copyright 1988 by

NATIONAL BUSINESS EDUCATION ASSOCIATION
1914 ASSOCIATION DRIVE
RESTON, VIRGINIA

$12.00

LIBRARY OF CONGRESS CARD No. 88-61094
ISBN 0-933964-27-7

Preface

Facilitating Communication for Business is an appropriate title for the National Business Education Association's 1988 Yearbook. It reflects not only the need for all businesspersons to enhance their communication skills but also the related opportunities for business educators to fulfill that need.

Part I of *Facilitating Communication for Business* discusses the importance of communication skills in the business world and identifies aspects of communication that businesspersons believe business educators ought to develop. Part II reviews the foundations of communication for business—listening, speaking, writing, and reading and organizational communication theory—and offers teaching-related suggestions. Part III suggests how business educators can improve their communication skill instruction by minimizing communication apprehension, by building communication skills with technologies, by increasing communication skills of nonnative speakers of English, and by developing intercultural communication skills for the global business community. Part IV provides business educators with information about appropriate curriculums and methodologies at the secondary school level, at the postsecondary level, at the undergraduate level, and at the graduate level. Part V integrates themes from the preceding chapters and urges all business educators to work cooperatively to develop communication skills for business.

This Yearbook represents a cross section of thought about how business educators can facilitate communication for business. It merits in-depth reading. Chapter authors are representatives of business and industry, specialists in various facets of communication, and business educators at all instructional levels. Some of the chapter authors are nationally known for such things as their contributions to the professional literature and their leadership in business communication circles; others, while not yet nationally known, are experts in their own communities. The balance among authors is further enhanced by author representation from throughout the United States.

Although it is impossible to name all of those who have contributed in one way or another to this Yearbook, I acknowledge with gratitude the cooperation and support of the members of the National Business Education Association's Executive Board, Publications Committee, and national headquarters staff; the authors of the various yearbook chapters; and the head, faculty, and staff of the Department of Administrative Systems and Business Education at Utah State University.

It is my sincere desire that *Facilitating Communication for Business* will serve as an impelling force that motivates all business educators to accept and to fulfill responsibilities for facilitating communication for business.

James Calvert Scott, Editor

Contents

PART IV. APPLICATIONS:
CURRICULUMS AND METHODOLOGIES

PART V. CONCLUSION:
A TIME FOR ACTION

Part I

INTRODUCTION: ESSENTIAL COMMUNICATION SKILLS

CHAPTER 1

The Importance of Communication Skills In the Business World

GAIL C. BROSTROM
Northern States Power Company, Minneapolis, Minnesota

The first career job: a major report to research, organize, and write; three very important meetings for which to prepare agendas and contact participants by memo; a special visitor who wants a tour of the department and a review of products and services; a crisis on another project with an update required by the manager through electronic mail; an in-house course on budgeting . . . all the first week!

Besides good time management skills, patience, and perseverance (all *not* the main topic of this article), communication skills are a top priority in accomplishing the described tasks. As a business worker and communicator, you are being asked to think, plan, communicate in writing or verbally, and take responsibility for accomplishing these tasks.

Communication skills needed in the business world are as varied as the tasks assigned to employees. Basically, workers must present a favorable image that other employees use to form an opinion of a department and that the public uses to form an opinion of the company as a whole. Business workers must be able to discuss verbally—in either formal or informal settings—their work assignments; they must be able to organize and write letters, memos, reports, and variations of those forms of communication; and they must be able to interact with co-workers with courtesy, consideration, and understanding.

Preparing students to meet the demands of a career position is a major responsibility of each of us. In 1984 the Policies Commission for Business and Economic Education challenged business educators to develop students' business communication skills.[1] Are we accepting that challenge? As stated by Kotler and Hickey, "the ultimate aim—for all of us—is to teach inexperienced writers that what they say publicly has important consequences for themselves and for those they address."[2]

Discussion in this article centers on the important communication skills required in business that have been identified through observation and

---

[1] Policies Commission for Business and Economic Education. "This We Believe About the Teaching of Business Communication." *Business Education Forum* 39:11; October 1984.

[2] Kotler, Janet, and Hickey, Dona. "Let's Call the Whole Thing Off." *Journal of Business Communication* 24:13; Winter 1987.

1

experience. Classroom activities that could be used to focus on these skills are also presented.

Communication is business, and business is communication. As indicated in the vignette, many communication tasks may be assigned to a business worker. As business educators we must emphasize to our students the importance of being able to communicate well on the job. In Bennett and Olney's study, over 84 percent of responding business people said communication skills had a major effect on advancement.[3] That's a *major* effect. Being able to communicate in any form also provides the students (soon-to-be-employees) with the confidence to assume tasks and see those tasks through to completion.

My basic premise is that with communication skills in their "back pocket" business workers are:

- Knowledgeable and educated
- Aware of the need to avoid wasting time
- Conscious of a professional, business image
- Valuable employees in the view of supervisors and co-workers
- Caring people because of the ability to analyze audiences
- Conscious of the trust placed in them by their employers
- Able to get their points across concisely and clearly using multiple forms of communication
- At an advantage over others who do not have the communication skills necessary to succeed.

COMMUNICATION ACTIVITIES IN BUSINESS

Experience in the classroom and observations in business have highlighted the need for certain communication skills. Here are the most common activities identified as important concerns in business. They are categorized and presented under four pertinent areas of business communication: *general,* including basic skills and audience analysis; *written,* including organization, style, and project development; *verbal,* including listening and presenting; and *interpersonal,* the unique skill.

General. The two skills discussed in the general category are basic skills and audience analysis.

BASIC SKILLS. Basic skills for verbal and written tasks are the "meat" of teaching. Without basic skills—spelling, punctuation, grammatical structure, and paragraph development—employees have no basis with which to develop other communication skills.

How very disheartening to read a report written by an "educated" person who has no regard for correct grammatical usage. Or, how embarrassed we feel when someone gives a verbal presentation using incomplete sentence structure, slang terminology, incorrect verb tenses, or colloquial expressions.

You may think no one—let alone upper management—has the time to

---

[3]Bennett, James C., and Olney, Robert J. "Executive Priorities for Effective Communication in an Information Society." *Journal of Business Communication* 23:15; Spring 1986.

attend to these details. This is not true; the details are noticed, and an impression is formed. True, a second attempt to improve may be given, but people have to know where to improve before doing so. We, then, as business communication instructors, must take the responsibility—no matter what grade level—of teaching, or reteaching, basic skills.

Granted, time in the classroom is limited because of many important subjects to cover. But business educators have many choices to make when teaching the how's and why's of basic skills. One choice would be to hear what local business people expect from new employees. This activity has always worked; experts seem more plausible than the instructors with whom students have day-to-day contact. Also, any grammatical review helps students with their relearning or applying basic skills. Even with the advent of computers offering spell checks, students still need to know basic skill requirements. In a local computer newspaper, the editor states, "English composition is the shop class of tomorrow. As communication becomes the marketable skill, English grammar and enunciation become more important."[4]

AUDIENCE ANALYSIS. The major point of audience analysis is that people never know where their reports and/or oral presentations may end up on the hierarchic ladder. If the supervisor/manager likes a report, it may be given to the director or general manager. If this is a possible result, why not construct and write a report for that possibility? All of us would prefer to be well prepared when asked to give a presentation on a topic that we researched. We need to assist our students in identifying all possible audience levels and what is expected from business workers when they are asked to write or present.

By the instructor establishing the ground rules for the audience, the students then have a basis for directing their writing and speaking. For example, a memo report on a research topic is directed to the department manager. The manager, in turn, directs the report to the general manager, who also has an interest in the research topic. Because of that interest, the general manager requests the employee (student) to present a synopsis of the report to other managers. This is a very typical route for new topics or new developments affecting departments in businesses.

Of course, more traditional forms of audiences may also be identified in the classroom. These could include a person requesting information on company products or a person needing explanations for a late delivery or a billing charge. The more detail given for each communication situation, the better students can imagine the end recipient of a speech or piece of writing.

Written. Three very important communication skills—organization, style, and project development—are associated with writing in business.

ORGANIZATION. Thinking, outlining, thinking, revising, researching, analyzing, thinking, revising . . . all contribute to the first and final organization of a written project. Here's where the knowledge of the audience and the topic are large components of success. Most managers are so inundated with

---

[4]Archibald, Dale. "Office Automation: In the Beginning Is the Word." *ComputerUser* 5:1; September 1986.

paper reports that time is of the essence when reading. The organization of a report, then, is extremely important.

Managers pay attention to first paragraphs, first sentences, and active voice. That's not to say they aren't interested in supporting material. However, wading through many paragraphs or pages to find the main point just isn't a luxury that many managers have. When organizing a report, these factors become a major consideration.

A direct approach of organizing and writing is most often expected when communicating upward, laterally, or downward. An indirect method, however, is used when the writer or speaker has news that may not be appreciated or understood by the audience. Using the indirect method is an excellent approach when explanations or supporting material must come before the main point.

Students need to distinguish when and how to use a logical (indirect) or psychological (direct) approach. Murphy and Peck use these terms to explain organizing a memo or longer report:

1. Logical pattern (introduction, text, and terminal section [summary, conclusions, recommendations])
2. Psychological pattern
   a. Organized by usual psychological pattern (terminal section before or after the introduction but always before the text)
   b. Organized by unusual pattern (purpose, cost and savings, conclusions, and discussion).[5]

When organizing any writing or speaking assignment, these two approaches are very appropriate. Of course, variations exist on the logical/psychological theme. When training students to organize, present the options. With two methods described to them and the particular assignment worked out in both, students can appreciate when and where to use each to best advantage.

STYLE. Style in writing business projects is as individual as fingerprints. However, business workers are often forced to acquire someone else's style while in the classroom or on the job. This happens mainly because business workers have not had a chance to develop their own sense of style. John S. Fielden in his often read article, "What Do You Mean You Don't Like My Style?" defines style as:

. . . that choice of words, sentences, and paragraph format which by virtue of being appropriate to the situation and to the power positions of both writer and reader produces the desired reaction and result.[6]

My recommendation to students in the classroom and business workers is to adjust their style to the situation. They must use the commonsense side of the brain and project themselves into the reader's role when determining style. As instructors, we can assist inexperienced writers by sharing examples of styles used by co-workers, supervisors, family, and friends. For example, your style may include a numbered response to a customer's request; another's

---

[5]Murphy, Herta, and Peck, Charles E. *Effective Business Communications.* New York: McGraw-Hill Book Co., 1972. p. 634.

[6]Fielden, John S. "What Do You Mean You Don't Like My Style?" *Harvard Business Review* 60:128; May-June 1982.

style may be to respond by paragraphing the responses using fourth-degree headings. Both may be effective, but the writer's style and analysis of the audience may be the deciding point on which approach to use. Neither style is incorrect; it's an opportunity to be as individual as possible using all techniques of writing and to discover appropriateness in any situation.

PROJECT DEVELOPMENT. Project development in writing tasks is an interesting concept that has become a necessity in the business world. In almost every business project, more than one piece of writing is required. Projects do not end with the sending of a report. They may continue for months with initial reports, progress reports, verbal reviews, suggestions, new research information, and then an updated final report.

My intrigue with project development is how to realistically incorporate the time frames and requirements into the classroom. Many opportunities arise in the classroom to include project development. One, in particular, is to initiate a business research project early in the schedule. Some ideas are electronic mail, local area networks, pros and cons of a new personnel policy such as early retirement, or review of competition in a chosen field.

The beginning of the project would be to initiate the research on a given topic by finding current articles and scheduling a due date for an annotated bibliography. The next step would include scheduling progress reports on what's been located, the source of the articles, and any problems encountered. While the research stage is evolving, classroom content can focus on report structure, organization, style, audience analysis, and differences between analytical and information reports.

Teachers can adapt the project development plan according to the length of class time (e.g., nine weeks, quarter, semester). Request letters can be written and sent; speeches can be made; guest speakers on chosen topics can be brought into the classroom. Any adjustments to the project—illness, change of command, redirection of the project—can be interjected for more reality, but time would be the deciding factor. The project development or management theme in the classroom is a realistic approach to the business world and an excellent transition skill.

Verbal. The verbal skills of listening and presenting are very often part of a communication curriculum. They are discussed here to emphasize the importance of both.

LISTENING. Listening skills in business as in personal life allow insight into meanings and messages. In Bennett and Olney's study, listening was one of the top five skills listed as a common problem by respondents. In fact, over 60 percent of the respondents listed poor listening skills as a top problem area.[7]

There are two ways to listen—passive and active. The image of a passive listener is graphically depicted by the "Live and Let Live" type described in an article in *Data Training:* "You just stand there and do your talking, and I'll just sit here and do my listening."[8]

---

[7]Bennett, James C., and Olney, Robert J. "Executive Priorities for Effective Communications in an Information Society." *Journal of Business Communication* 23:17; Spring 1986.

[8]News and Trends. "Trainees To Watch Out For." *Data Training* 6:6; February 1987.

Being a passive listener will most likely frustrate a business worker. When receiving work instruction, the passive listener will react according to known assumptions and comparisons. With these impressions, the passive listener begins and completes a work assignment that may have no bearing on what was expected.

Our task is to convert the passive listener to an active listener, one who will become involved in the listening process and receive many benefits from having active involvement. An active listener is physically and mentally involved in the process. In a discussion of how perceptions or personal ability affect an individual's assumption and, therefore, distortion of what is heard, Switzer defines active listening as focusing on the other person—to understand what the other person's reality is and what is really being said.[9]

An active listener uses acquired skills that focus on what is expected. These skills involve (1) asking appropriate questions, (2) jotting associated thoughts alongside notes so that appropriate questions can be asked, (3) paraphrasing what is heard, (4) restating if any misunderstanding occurs, and (5) summarizing the instructions at the conclusion. The use of these skills will benefit all involved—supervisors and business workers. The image of an active listener is that of a person who is interested, content oriented, concerned about the outcome, and eager to explore options.

PRESENTING. Presentation skills in business rely on two themes—content and process. Switzer defines content as being "the explicit information being transmitted" and process as being "how a message is sent: tone of voice, body language, and the hidden or implicit messages that may be present."[10] These themes occur in any communication situation but are referenced here as they pertain to presentations. Those presentations may be given to supervisors, department members, senior management, or external professional organizations.

A business worker must be prepared to present at any time, most often on a known subject but sometimes on an unfamilar topic. Imagine being a new employee asked to present a summary of findings to department managers. The summary is from a report on which you spent many weeks and is of great interest to the managers. You have 10 minutes of their time, and your manager is expecting a job well done. What's involved?

Content: Known
Time and detail—limited
Input from manager on audience (of course, using active listening skills)

Process: Graphs/charts (presents information succinctly and eliminates audience staring at speaker)
Businesslike dress (to project the proper image)
Delivery (volume/tone control, nonquivering voice)
Presence (using body language to match the expectations of the audience)

Subject knowledge is a major point in presentations, but presence may be one of the most important for novice—even experienced—speakers. What

---

[9]Switzer, Alan L. "Contact and Clout: Developing Communication Skills." *Words* 13:30; October-November 1984.
[10]*Ibid.*, p. 29.

types of habits must a novice speaker break before acquiring presence? A novice speaker, out of nervousness, may giggle. A novice speaker may end a statement with a question. Novice speakers may slouch, stand with their hands in their pockets, lean on the podium, or stand in front of the transparencies or slides. These speakers may rely on "you know" or "okay" to fill the thought process. The audience, in the meantime, observes and makes judgments based on impressions formed during the presentations. What a dilemma!

The good news is that these are all breakable habits. By breaking these habits before entering the business world, business workers will have the confidence to present to any group. This increases the positive image of the individuals, their supervising managers, and their department.

The experience required for public presentations can be obtained from most classroom activities, social gatherings, or extracurricular events. Allen, from a survey of 1,000 executives, suggested that students participate in symposium and panel discussions to improve presentation skills. The executives felt students should prepare "adequately for presentations on short notice, as well as make the actual delivery."[11] Business educators should provide students with opportunities to practice presentation skills. After all, the more practice students receive, the easier the transition will be to business situations.

Interpersonal. Interpersonal skills are considered unique since they are so dependent on the individual. Because they involve more personal contact with people, they are different to some degree than written or verbal skills. Yet they are crucial for business workers—a major component that makes a business operate effectively. No one works in a void; people at work have goals, dreams, and their own way of getting a job done.

The importance of good interpersonal skills is demonstrated in a discussion by Stiegler of why people are terminated from jobs. It's not "because of lack of specialized knowledge and skills, but because of not being able to interact effectively with co-workers and managers." In fact, over 70 percent of people who lose their jobs do so for this reason.[12] Smeltzer and Gebert found in a survey of graduates from agriculture, business, engineering, and physical sciences that interpersonal communication received top priority among all four professions.[13] Interestingly, the respondents spent approximately 14 percent, 6 percent, and 39 percent of their time in informal group discussions, formal group meetings, and face-to-face communication, respectively. The implications are that interpersonal functions are a very common occurrence in business—and an important basis for keeping a job.

Business workers will share their day with others who have different perceptions, assumptions, and goals. What do employers want from these diverse groups of people? They want people who are "team players" yet individual in the sense of assuming responsibility and completing tasks. Being

---

[11]Allen, Thomas R., Jr. "Business Leaders Stress Communication Skills." *Balance Sheet* 68:5; January-February 1987.

[12]Stiegler, C. B. "Human Interaction . . . Efficient and Effective Sharing of Information." *Secretary* 44:22; March 1984.

[13]Smeltzer, Larry R., and Gebert, Kaylene A. "How Business Communication Needs Differ Among Professions." *Bulletin of the Association for Business Communication* 49:7; September 1986.

a team player means that a business worker is striving to achieve department goals, supervisors' goals, and corporate goals. Activity as a team player will involve a great amount of sharing information, forming strategy to complete tasks, and analyzing end results of a project.

Certain individuals will assume responsibility to complete parts of or all of a work task to meet a goal. Employers expect those individuals to complete a job with maturity, common sense, and direction. They also expect those individuals to use the other skills that have been previously discussed.

The uniqueness of interpersonal relationships is the individual. Not everyone works quite the same way or achieves goals in the same manner. What future business workers should understand is how they perform assignments and set goals compared to other people. What frustrates them when working with other people? What do they like to see when they and their family or friends go out to conduct business?

These questions plus many others can be asked and reviewed in the classroom. The responses should indicate to students what business expects from them. Such matters should be discussed in the classroom because once students are employed their employers will expect them to perform according to standards.

Human relations has long been a topic in business classes. The use of human relations skills affects all professions and should be practiced as writing and speaking are practiced. Some excellent textbooks are available that offer exercises in conflict, group work, values, and taking direction. They have activities that help students understand how people react to different situations and give them perspectives that will help on the job.

Interpersonal relationships, human relations, business cooperation—whatever it is called, it is an important area of communication. With good interpersonal skills, business workers can learn how to work successfully with many groups of people and levels of supervisors.

COMMUNICATION ACTIVITIES IN THE CLASSROOM

There are many classroom activities that can be used to help students acquire the previously discussed skills. These, as well as the ones mentioned earlier, are not all inclusive; rather they can be incorporated into all business communication assignments.

Simulations. One major curriculum component is the business simulation used along with the regular textbook. A simulation that identifies a specific business with related writing, speaking, and interpersonal tasks works best.

The advantages of using simulations are:

1. Students identify with one company as they do when working.

2. Students can perform a variety of tasks while becoming familiar with samples of business functions.

3. Students have an opportunity to review others' work and rewrite or restructure assignments as they would when on the job.

4. Instructors can discuss all aspects of a business and include activities that simulate real-world requirements in addition to the simulation.

5. Instructors have the opportunity to structure the class around time limitations.

Some disadvantages are that simulations, especially product-oriented textbooks, are outdated quickly. This should not be discouraging, however, since activities can be done on suggested upgrading of the products. Another disadvantage may be the students' lack of business experience; instructors, then, may have to spend more time explaining business requirements and functions.

Most simulations give guidelines for any class level and time, which helps with instructors' planning. If the activities meet class objectives, then the simulation will work. The students acquire realistic situations from which to work, and with guidance, they can analyze, organize, and write accordingly.

Guest speakers. The use of outside speakers has long been an effective classroom activity. One of the most common reasons for guest speakers is for specialized tasks such as interviewing, communication expectations, specific writing projects, and preparing audiovisual aids for presentations.

However, as business educators, we could also use the guest speakers to support the theories of communication discussed in the classroom. For instance, after a guest speaker has presented the information and has left, we could question the students on aspects of presentations: What did you like about the manner of presentation? What didn't you like? What was the presence of the speaker? Would you be comfortable maintaining that presence? Why? Why not? If students are given the opportunity to gain knowledge on a particular subject, why not have them gain perspective on how different people use communication skills too?

Whether or not to inform guest speakers of the postpresentation activities would be up to the teacher. Speakers may be very interested in the evaluation, especially if they are relatively new to public presentations. The evaluation would not be a personal attack but would be a chance to evaluate many ways of presenting information.

Guest speakers often provide the incentive and motivation for students who are difficult to stimulate in the day-to-day contact with the instructor. Using guest speakers is also an opportunity for students to become familiar with their community and its business activities.

Assignment details. When using the cases in textbooks, we often assume all the information is presented. However, many students will not understand the complete situation and thus feel inadequate when trying to write.

My proposal is that we give them more detail and information when assigning these cases. For example, what are the ramifications to the business if a direct letter is written in a bad-news situation? Will it result in loss of a customer? Better understanding by the client? A telephone call to the writer's supervisor? Rather than just write, students should realize the consequences of how they choose to write.

Explanation of the audience expectations and what the business can do are two topics that can be applied to case studies. Details on assignments enhance the understanding of students. When they learn to analyze alternatives, then students can apply all communication skills.

Who benefits from this application of communication skills? Both the students when they are employed and the businesses employing them are the benefactors. Of course, we benefit, too. When students are able to communicate better and with more understanding, they will more closely meet our expectations and lessen our frustration.

CONCLUSION

Students must know what businesses expect of them. Businesses want more than mediocre employees. Mediocrity is common; excellence is the distinctive quality. Possessing communication skills and transferring them to business applications benefits both employees and employing businesses. Communication skills and resulting job performance are truly the keys to success in the business world.

Part II
FOUNDATIONS: PERSPECTIVES ON COMMUNICATION

CHAPTER 2

Developing Basic Listening Skills

NORMA COSTNER
Riverwood High School, Atlanta, Georgia

Listening is the part of communication that must not be taken for granted. It is not an inate ability. Teachers have to be alert to listening habits or to the lack of listening that students exhibit in their classes and include drill and practice designed to improve these skills. Education cannot occur without effective listening.

WHAT IS LISTENING?

The ability to listen should not be confused with the ability to hear. Hearing is dependent on the ears. Listening uses the mind and the eyes as well. With one's mind one is able to perceive the message, interpret the meaning, and react to it. With the eyes one is able to perceive the nonverbal cues that are a major part of the communicated message. Listening requires concentration, critical analysis, and empathy with the message. How many times might one hear every word someone else says in a long conversation or speech but be unable to repeat even a hazy account of what was said? This describes a passive activity that appears to be listening, but it is not comprehension. This type of listening applied in a situation where it makes a difference produces no valuable results.

Most people view listening as a passive activity: someone speaks and someone else listens. In this situation the audience has the option of paying attention part of the time or not at all. They can tune in or tune out at will. This is not listening. Listening is active involvement with the speaker.

IMPORTANCE OF LISTENING

Sociologists and pyschologists have identified communication as the most important element in human interaction. It is required in learning situations, business transactions, and personal friendships. Communication is the major factor in building all human relationships. These include business relationships between managers and employees; personal relationships among co-workers, family, and spouse; and educational relationships between teachers and students. Ineffective communication adversely affects work production, morale, and the family foundation because people in every situation are insecure when they are functioning under "fuzzy shoulds." It is important to communicate the "shoulds" clearly and to listen to the "shoulds" effectively.

11

Counselors report that personal relationships are built on a clear understanding of each person's needs; educators believe that good education occurs when there is clarity of instruction and rapport between teachers and students; managers show that management by communicating objectives increases productivity. The benefits of listening are many—including increased knowledge, friendships, job opportunities, promotions, and improved language usage.

Approximately one-third of a person's waking hours are spent listening either in school, in social interactions, at home, or on the job. Listening is well over half of any communication process although many think that other communications skills such as speaking, reading, and writing are more important. There is a tendency to think it is what one says that is important, not necessarily what one hears. This is confirmed by the amount of time educators spend developing reading, writing, and speaking skills compared to the small amount of time educators spend emphasizing listening. Because of this hierarchy of communication skills, little or nothing is included in the curriculum of any discipline to improve listening.

Most people take listening for granted. Even though few rate listening as important as reading, writing, and speaking, one spends more time listening than engaged in any of the other communication activities. More than half of communication involves listening; but when one includes the time spent in front of the television or other media listening to programming and presentations, the percentage may be higher.

When children enter elementary school, they are taught to read, write, recognize sounds, and comprehend. In addition, they are evaluated as to whether they listen well enough. Frequently children are admonished for demonstrating poor listening in their early years in elementary school. But is there any planned training in elementary school to improve listening other than to define it as a behavior problem? The failure of young people to listen is probably the number one complaint of parents and teachers. This is a valid concern because of the amount of time students spend listening and the influence listening has on success. Frequently a student fails a course not because of the inability to learn but because of poor listening. An employee may be fired because of the inability to listen and follow through on instruction, not because of poor job skills. Children with an attention span deficit can be helped by training in listening techniques, in classroom drill, and the use of other behavior modification techniques, as well as medical treatment for the condition.

In high school as many as 9 out of every 10 hours in classes are devoted to lecture and discussion. Most of a student's exposure to learning is through listening—discussions, lectures, directions, and instruction. The average high school student earning an academic diploma attends approximately 2,000 lectures in his or her high school career and another 2,000 lectures in college. This emphasizes the need for improving listening skills.

Listening to 50 or 60 minutes of instruction is a difficult task. Casual attentiveness is not effective. Casual listening may be acceptable for social interaction, but in an instructional forum it is necessary to remember the essential details and to comprehend the main ideas. Instruction is usually a one-time opportunity. One can always read something again, but one cannot listen twice.

When students enter high school, many have developed such poor listening habits that they don't attempt to pay attention or to listen until the teacher has repeated the instruction several times. This makes the task of teaching content an obligation to undo bad listening habits before learning can occur. The place to start is in preschool or in elementary school when all other communication skills are introduced. If teachers could double the average listening proficiency and retention from 25 to 50 percent, consider what this would mean in relation to students' learning, social lives, and jobs.

TYPES OF LISTENING

There are two types of listening: casual, informal and active, formal listening. Casual, informal listening is only intense enough to absorb as many of the speaker's remarks as are needed to keep a conversation going. One can get by with that because one is not expected to give a verbatim account or take a test on the content. It really doesn't matter whether one remembers the exact details or not. Because there is so much of this kind of listening, most people are inclined to neglect the development of active, formal listening skills that are necessary in almost all other situations.

Active listening calls for concentrating, absorbing, and fixing in the mind as many of the details as possible. It requires active participation and thinking. Active listening is required of the student in learning and of the employee in job performance. It is vital for the doctor in listening to the patient, the salesman in assessing the needs of the consumer, the telephone operator in placing calls, the sales clerk in finding the correct size, the policeman in making accurate reports, and the lawyer in establishing evidence and details of a case. For many people, listening is the difference between career success or failure.

Both types of listening involve activity of the mind. The listener must reach out to empathize and catch what is in the mind of the speaker. There must be a willingness to listen and to learn from the speaker. Cognitive listening is concerned with evaluating the information—not the speaker. One must be involved to the point of being able to put the information in sequence and in context with a personal situation. If it is appropriate, clarify misunderstandings. Ask questions such as, Do I understand you to mean . . .? Confirming what one hears by restating the main points is an example of self-initiated involvement.

Cognitive listening also involves perceiving nonverbal cues which influence communication as much as the spoken word. There is truth to the statement, "It's not what you say; it's how you say it." A significant part of the message is obtained from nonverbal cues such as posture, facial expressions, tone of voice, appearance, eye contact, and rapport with the audience. These cues can be used to enhance listening skills if perceived correctly. (However, if they are too extreme, they can be barriers. Pay attention to these cues, but conscientiously avoid being distracted by them.)

13

BARRIERS TO LISTENING

Cognitive, active listening requires one to block out barriers that interfere with comprehension. It means overcoming the obstacles to listening such as distracting mannerisms, environmental distractions, letting the mind wander, overreacting to emotional subjects, or daydreaming. The listener cannot change the mannerisms and physical appearance of the speaker, but he/she can control personal reactions to them by being aware that some traits may be distracters. The listener can also control other internal obstacles that interfere with good listening. Among these obstacles are the following:

1. Listening with a judging, prejudiced attitude—believing that it is necessary to approve or disapprove, judging based on personal likes and dislikes

2. Thinking about oneself and giving a response as soon as the opportunity arises

3. Assuming what the speaker is going to say, that it is unimportant, and then tuning out

4. Hearing what one wants to hear, ignoring what one disagrees with or feels threatened by

5. Faking attentiveness and daydreaming

6. Prejudging the speaker or the content and closing one's mind to new ideas

7. Paying too much attention to the speaker's appearance, pronunciation, accent, voice, mannerisms, and grammar.

To be an effective listener, try to overcome personal irritants—concentrate on the message, not on the person or personal prejudices. Barriers that interfere with good listening can be overcome by controlling concentration through a willingness and conscientious effort to listen. In addition, if one can control his or her own body language and posture, this will enhance effective listening and comprehension.

Body posture is important and can subconsciously improve or deter listening. Improve listening by facing the speaker. Lean toward the speaker to show attentiveness and willingness to be an active participant. Give the speaker eye contact at least 80 percent of the time. Watch your hands. Writers on the subject of body language report that there are recognized signals that are interpreted in certain ways. Negative examples are folded arms, closed arms, steepling with one's hands, and leaning back in the chair. Positive examples are open arms, relaxed hands, and leaning forward. These signals communicate attitudes to the speaker and to oneself. Attitude does affect listening; therefore, manage body posture.

Eliminate behaviors that distract the speaker and interfere with listening. Don't interrupt. One cannot listen if time is spent thinking about the response and then interrupting to say it. Don't be afraid to let silence fall between a question or comment before responding. Allow time to think during this pause instead of preparing a response ahead of time and then interrupting. Don't fidget or look around the room. This allows external stimuli to interfere with the communication. If it is a one-on-one conversation, respond to the speaker with a nod or some signal to show interest.

HOW TO LISTEN IN CONVERSATION—THE DIALOGUE

Some conversations are relatively unimportant, and it is not really critical whether one listens effectively or not. In other two-way conversations such as the job interview or the informal sales presentation, listening is crucial.

When participating in conversations, as when listening to speeches, one tends to be distracted although perhaps not as easily. In conversation the barriers to listening are more likely to be one's own natural tendency to judge, to evaluate, and to approve or disapprove of the person or his/her ideas. All of these attitudes tend to get in the way of listening to the other person's point of view. One is always agreeing or disagreeing or making some judgment. These barriers to communication on a personal level are intensified when feelings and emotions are deeply involved. The stronger the feelings, the more likely it is that one will become self-centered and there will be no communication. Emotions are the principal barrier to communication in a personal relationship. Real communication occurs when there is listening with understanding. This means to listen with the attitude of seeing the issue from the other person's point of view, to sense how that person feels about it and to understand his or her frame of reference. Becoming a better listener can alter a person's basic personality and improve relationships with others.

Some people are reluctant to become good listeners because listening with understanding and concentration is risky. They run the risk of being changed, having to let go of old ideas. Because of this, they resist listening too carefully. It is safer to listen with an evaluative attitude because listening with an open mind would seem too threatening to an established set of values. Simply hearing what one wants to hear is more comfortable. A breakdown in communications and the evaluative tendency are the major barriers to true listening and can be avoided if the desire is there.

HOW TO PARTICIPATE ACTIVELY IN LISTENING

Listening, like any other activity, is only effective when the listener is actively participating. Developing good listening habits is something one must do personally. Teachers can make students aware of the importance of listening and expose them to some of the drill and practice necessary to develop listening skills; but because listening is a voluntary activity, the incentive to listen must come from the listener.

Active listening requires a desire to listen by the listener, bringing to the situation an open mind free of prejudices and distracters. The active listener concentrates on what the speaker is saying. Most listeners can listen at a rate four times faster than speakers can talk; therefore, it is easy to spend this lag time on distractions or daydreaming. This causes the listener to be lost when he/she attempts to return attention to the lecture or discussion.

To avoid getting lost, the listener should think along with the speaker. The listener should find something to do with the lag time. Taking notes, particularly when listening to a speech or a lecture, keeps one actively involved with the subject under discussion.

HOW TO LISTEN TO A SPEECH

Listening to a speech requires active participation, and taking notes forces one to participate. Effective note-taking requires preparation of two sets of notes—one while the speech is being delivered, the other after the speech has ended. The first set is a paraphrased account of the delivery; the second set is a summary including reactions, opinions, and questions.

When listening to a speech, first know what kind of speech it is. Is it a sales speech to persuade, an instructional speech to improve the mind by adding knowledge, or a self-help speech to affect conduct as in a sermon? In all cases, keep attentive for "silver bullets," the statements that are the gist and the main points. Write these down. Also, write down what the speaker says is important. Listen for the speaker's assumptions and conclusions. Record these, too.

When the speech ends, summarize it. Combine the first set of notes along with memory, adding the details remembered but not recorded. Record reactions. What part of the speech is accurate, and what part is inaccurate? Which ideas are agreeable or not? Write down what is not understandable. Pose questions.

When listening to a speech, one must be more careful to block out any interference with comprehension than in informal communication. It is easier to succumb to outside influences when listening in a passive setting. Keep on task by doing something related to the speech, such as note-taking.

ROLE OF NOTE-TAKING

Reports state that retention is only 50 percent of what is heard immediately after hearing it. Two months later, one has forgotten another 25 percent, leaving only 25 percent retention. This makes good notes necessary since they are the only permanent record of the important ideas.

Good listening and good note-taking go together. The process of taking notes forces the listener to participate actively. Active listening, on the other hand, is required for one to make good notes.

A good listener takes notes in the sequence in which information is presented. This must be done with discretion, however. If a listener spends too much time taking notes, it is easy to miss the message or substitute note-taking for active listening. Take critical notes after listening, organizing the points in whatever order meets personal needs. Do not jot down reactions during the initial phase of note-taking—save these reactions for the second set of notes to be prepared after the speech has ended. A listener tends to get too involved in personal opinions and thoughts and misses some points if both are attempted at the same time.

Speaking and silent listening seldom serve the purpose of communication. Through note-taking and organizing notes, one can respond and become involved in the communication.

16

TEACHING LISTENING SKILLS IN BUSINESS EDUCATION

Business educators, perhaps more than teachers in any other discipline, are in a prime position to teach all communication skills. This is true because of the emphasis on communication included in all areas of the business curriculum.

Business communication is a course especially designed to teach reading, writing, speaking, and listening skills. Shorthand is another course that requires effective listening and writing skills. Hearing, listening, and retention are precisely the skills to be developed. Most students are able to memorize the outlines in a relatively short period of time and possess sufficient motor skill to write them fast enough. However, the skills that require endless drill are listening and processing what is heard. It is these skills that are in demand by businesses when they require shorthand as a job prerequisite. Notehand is a course which integrates a shortened writing system such as shorthand or speedwriting with the skills related to listening and the production of useful notes for study. Vocational office training and other office occupations courses include communication skills because the development of a successful employee is dependent upon listening and following through on the assigned tasks.

All other business courses can include listening as an integrated part of the curriculum. These courses as well as every other course in the high school or college curriculum are as much a development of good habits as the direct application of the course work. Teachers who "spoon feed" and continue to repeat the same instructions encourage sloppy listening. Teachers who command attention and place some of the burden upon students for at least hearing, if not understanding, the content have taken one step in the right direction toward emphasizing good listening skills. Teachers of any subject on any grade level can recognize the need for listening and comprehension and incorporate listening drills into the classwork.

EXERCISES TO IMPROVE LISTENING

For a long time businesses have recognized the increased productivity when employees are able to read rapidly; therefore, they have included speed reading training in staff development seminars. Recently some corporations have added listening training to these programs. The rationale for this emphasis is based on the beliefs that listening is in fact a communication skill and that efficient listening is just as important in improving communication between managers and employees as any other skill.

So important are habits of good listening that large corporations such as AT&T, General Motors, General Electric, Xerox, Coca Cola, IBM, and others offer listening inservice training to their executives and supervisory personnel. They have developed programs because of an increasing need for clear communications between the employees and employers as well as between the company and the public. These companies believe that managers must know how to listen if they are to be effective. Most companies tailor their inservice training to the needs identified by the departments. Listening is frequently identified as the skill most needed to increase profits or productivity. Many believe the best salesmen are the best listeners, not the best speakers.

Some of the inservice activities used by these companies can be integrated into any class where a part of the curriculum requires speaking and listening. For example, here are some activities used in listening seminars at Coca Cola.

1. *Diagnostic Listening Test—Repeat Verbatim.* Divide into groups of two. The first person speaks for 10 seconds while the other person listens. After 20 seconds have lapsed, the listener repeats verbatim what the speaker said.

2. *Diagnostic Listening Test—Rumor Clinic.* Five people are sent out of the room. The rest of the group are given two handouts. The first handout is a written passage. The second handout is a page to record deletions and additions. The people sent out of the room are called in one at a time. The first person reads the passage and relays as much of it as can be recalled to the next person returning to the room. One by one those returning listen and repeat as much of the passage as possible to the next one. The last person repeats it to the group, at which point it is determined how much of the original passage is left.

3. *Attending Exercise.* Attending is actually listening and observing the speaker. This exercise demonstrates the effect of not attending. Divide the class into groups of two. One will tell the other a story. The listener gives the speaker the obvious message that he or she is not listening—looks around the room, scatches a leg, looks at a watch, or the like. After behaving this way, the listener may then be asked to repeat what was heard. The point is to stress the effect inattentive behavior has on both the speaker and the listener.

4. *Focusing Exercise.* In this exercise, listeners are taught to focus on the main idea. Groups of two are organized. One person tells the other a story. When the speaker is finished, the listener says, "Let me get this right . . ." or "By this you mean . . ." or "You are saying that . . ." This requires the listener to restate, clarify or confirm the idea.

5. *Understanding Exercise.* Understanding is comprehending the total message, giving meaning to the message, and interpreting and evaluating the speaker's statement. This involves recall, identifying the feelings and content, and developing a personal notion of the message including evaluation or judgment. This sets the stage for responding. One exercise in differentiating between verbal responses and nonverbal responses could involve videotaping an interview between two people. After watching the videotape, have students list the responses of each person, labeling the responses as verbal or nonverbal.

6. *Responding Exercise.* Responding serves the primary purpose of reflecting what was heard. Clarification of what is heard encourages further communication. The response measures whether one has accurately interpreted the speaker's words and gives the speaker the opportunity to correct or clarify understanding. Among the clarifying responses are paraphrasing, summarizing, giving examples, requesting additional information, and reflecting. An activity in responding is to have one student give directions

to a particular place. The other student listens and then asks questions.

These listening components—attending, focusing, understanding, and responding—are all interrelated and take place within split seconds in the mind. The exercises will bring awareness of personal listening habits.

Other listening activities emphasize many elements of good listening that are appropriate for the classroom. Some of these activities include:

1. *Listening Diary.* Have students keep an estimated record of the listening activities in which they engage during one school day. Total the time spent listening. Compare results with classmates.

2. *Introduction Game.* Divide the class into groups of five or six. Each person assumes another name and introduces himself/herself. After all introductions are made determine how many students can reintroduce the members of their group.

3. *Role Play Job Interview.* Ask two students to role play an interview for a job. The applicant is to demonstrate poor listening techniques. Have the class list the listening distracters that occur during the interview.

4. *Listening Survey.* Have students evaluate their own listening effectiveness by having them answer a teacher-prepared listening questionnaire or one from a business communication textbook.

5. *Memory Retention Exercises.* Dictate a passage for a minute or two with the students listening. Then have the students write verbatim what was dictated. This is appropriate for shorthand or notehand classes.

6. *Read Short Article.* Read a short article to the class. Have students listen and then give an oral summary of the article.

CONCLUSION

The basic principles of listening should be applied in every situation. First, know why—listen with a purpose. Respond to the speaker in a positive way, discarding any personal or external distracters. Listen carefully to achieve understanding, and clarify points until understanding of the ideas is reached. Lay aside prejudices and take a chance on having personal ideas changed. Listen actively by focusing on what the speaker is saying, relating the facts and ideas to a personal situation, and sensing the nonverbal message of the speaker. Listen with empathy by trying to understand the speaker's position.

Efficient listening, like any other communication skill, requires drill and practice. Teachers have the obligation to make students aware of the need for good listening skills and to provide practice activities to develop them.

CHAPTER 3

Developing Basic Speaking Skills

JEAN S. GORDON

First Colonial High School, Virginia Beach, Virginia

Basic speaking skills are necessary for everyday activities as well as in delivering formal speeches. Most of the time these skills are used instinctively. Beginning with the moment of birth and its accompanying cry, virtually all behavior is accompanied by some act of inner or overt speech. As infants become conscious of being alive, as they become aware of physical changes and of their responses to them, as they begin to have needs, there is more vocalization. This vocalization is expressive, and the expressions of personality make their appearance. The happy baby reveals his or her happiness by contented sounds. The unhappy baby often cries.

As small children learn to use words, their physical activities are usually accompanied by speech. They play and talk aloud—to themselves and to others. They begin to entertain ideas and to work out problems. They express not only their wishes and feelings but their thinking as well. Their speech patterns indicate that intellectually, physically, and emotionally they are functioning as an integrated entity.

Children, as they gradually mature, reveal their development and growth through speech. Speech development reflects intellectual, physical, and emotional maturity—or the failure to mature. Almost all conscious behavior is accompanied by some form of speech. Consequently, speech—words and the way they are used—begins to represent adult behavior. Through the words and voices people hear, they form impressions of others they never see. Rightly or wrongly, people assume that others are as they are portrayed in speech.

Maturing individuals, with complexities of wants and wishes, have an increased need to use language in order to control their environment. Through speech individuals satisfy some of their wants and wishes. The personality that is revealed through speech is the result of a continuous process of growing. Though growth is a continuous process, it does not always progress at a smooth and even place. Speech develops and parallels intellectual, physical, and emotional growth. When the three aspects of growth are well integrated, speech and personality are well integrated.

Personality is the impression people make as a result of overt behavior. It is most readily expressed in speaking. Through speech people not only express personalities but also make adjustments and modifications of behavior which reflect growth and change. A person's language, voice, and gestures reveal an ability to succeed in the environment. A proper evaluation of speech, from the point of view of the speaker as well as from the listener, will prevent maladjustment. Sensitivity to the effects of speech behavior on others should help to modify undesirable personality traits. Few needs are as great as the need for communication, and few means of communication are as rewarding as speaking to or with others.

An understanding of the nature of human communication is a prerequisite to learning the specific principles and techniques that go into public speaking. The appreciation of the human interaction involved in speaking is basic to developing and delivering an effective speech.

PARTS OF THE SPEECH

A good speech has direction. The speaker should first identify/introduce the topic; second, deliver the message; and third, summarize the message. The informative speech then should have three major divisions: (1) an introduction, (2) a body, and (3) a conclusion.

Introduction. In the introductory portion of a speech, the speaker should accomplish three goals: first, secure the immediate attention of the audience and promote long range, continuous attention; second, explain exactly what the speech is about; third, provide a forecast of just why this information is of importance to the listener. During this beginning portion of the speech, speakers can establish a favorable rapport between themselves and their audience. Remember, first impressions count.

There are various techniques that speakers have at their disposal for a dynamic introduction. An excellent way for speakers to begin is to relate an appropriate personal experience. Everyone enjoys hearing what has happened to other people. Speakers may also begin by using quotations (literary or professional) if they will aid in explaining the importance of the topic. A third method of introduction involves using statistics. Facts and figures that reflect on the topic and are stated with authority can enhance introductory remarks. The rhetorical question also lends itself to an effective introduction. It is always provocative and serves as an attention catcher. The speaker simply raises a question that pinpoints the information in the speech; it is, of course, a question that the speaker does not expect to have answered by the listeners.

Body. This is the main portion of the speech where the speaker gives the audience the information promised in the introduction. In preparing this portion of the speech, the speaker must ask six questions about the topic: what? why? how? who? when? and where? However, in the presentation, he/she may not wish to cover *all* of these questions; the topic is the determining factor in deciding which one or two of these questions will be answered in the body of the speech.

Conclusion. The conclusion has three functions: (1) to provide a brief summary of the information presented; (2) to restate the importance of the information to effect an increased devotion to the speaker's idea; and (3) to close the speech with a strong sentence that leaves the audience in a receptive and positive frame of mind.

ORGANIZATION OF THE SPEECH

Now that the speaker has determined the structure of the speech, the task at hand is to organize the material for presentation. A main idea should be selected—good speeches say a few things well. Even if the speech is long, the time should be used to develop the main points rather than adding more points. Phrasing of the main idea deserves special attention because this is what the audience will remember long after the speech is made. The main idea should stand out and be concise. Main points should be parallel—this structure will make it easier for the audience to remember them.

Support the main idea—the more support given to this idea, the more believeable it is to the audience. Support can be in the form of facts, expert opinions, illustrations, specifics, or, perhaps, restatement.

SHAPING OF THE SPEECH

Strive to address the speech in such a manner that meaning will be instantly clear. If an impression is to be made at all, it must be done as the speech proceeds. If the speech is to be impressive, it must be instantly so. If it is to be meaningful, it must be meaningful at the moment the words are spoken. A first requisite, then, is clarity.

Make the speech clear. Choose words that are concrete, not general. The English language is extremely rich in synonyms, and there is no reason why they cannot be used to express meaning. Abstract words are for lazy people. The most useful words are specific verbs, nouns, and defining modifiers.

The verb is the motor of the sentence and does much to propel an idea. Use active, descriptive, lively verbs, rather than general ones.

The same is true of nouns. Take time to choose the specific noun over an abstract one. Under the term *cat* there are many kinds of interesting specimens. There is a kitten, lynx, tiger, spiteful woman, and heavy road equipment. Which term is appropriate for this speech?

Avoid the use of cluttering modifiers that just get in the way. "Very," "most," and "much" are the worst offenders here. Use instead defining modifiers that tell something the audience needs to know such as "old man," "warm day," "tiny stone."

Make the speech direct. Adapt language to personalities, to audiences, and to occasions. Adapt it to fit the personal speaker-audience relationship of speech. Do not fear using the personal language of talk, which is characterized by the frequent use of me, you, us, we, my, ours, and yours. Say "our United States," not "the United States"; "as you can see," not "as can be seen"; "note these points," not "it should be noted."

The good speaker uses short sentences because long and involved statements do not make for easy listening. However, variety does add interest.

Directness is also achieved by simplicity of language. Do not make the mistake of thinking that language has to be "dressed up" for formal speeches. The simple is often the most beautiful.

Make the speech vivid. Language can be personal, direct, and clear; but it may fail to be impressive. Most of the time, however, it does not need to be impressive. Everyday language suffices for daily thoughts and normal business. But if words are to be impressive and remembered, the vocabulary should be chosen realizing that it must be appropriate, it must be in good taste, and most important of all, it must be the speaker's own. In order to convey this, the speaker must be comfortable with the words even though he/she does not use them as everyday language.

Language that is direct, clear, and personal is of primary importance even though it may not be particularly impressive. It is always preferable to that which is artificial, pretentious, or insincere. If it is direct, clear, personal, and impressive, then the thoughts it expresses are much more likely to be remembered.

Some words hinder. Language may both help and hinder the ability of speakers to convey thoughts to their audience. When words are worn-out or trite, artificial or pretentious, they form a barrier between speaker and audience, and they block communication. Effective speakers will attempt to improve their speeches by getting rid of all cliches and worn-out expressions.

Use effective transitions. Speeches, like highways, need signposts to help listeners see where the speech is going. Take special care to keep listeners posted on the relationships of the ideas that are expressed. Transitions tell the audience where it has been, where it is now, and where it is going. For example: Now that we have . . . let us consider . . .; since we have seen . . . it is not at all surprising that . . .; not only . . . but also. . . .

CONTENT VERSUS PRESENTATION

Presentation is more important than content—unfortunately. If listeners enjoy a presentation, they are hardly conscious of whether the content of that presentation was of any great value. But the reverse is not true—the most valuable content will not salvage a poor presentation. Mastery of subject is a most important asset, but speakers still need to be good presenters.

Obstacles to good presentations include fear. This causes a dry throat, moist palms, fluttery stomach, nausea, a struggle for breath, feet that feel like lead weights, and the like. Another obstacle is lack of self-confidence. This obstacle includes the fear of failing, appearing inadequate, appearing the fool, and being embarrassed. The real obstacle, though, is the fear of being naked— not literally, of course—but exposed, defenseless, vulnerable, since all eyes are on the speaker.

To feel less naked, if possible, a speaker may sit behind a table with several other people (as in a panel discussion with informal speaking) or use a lectern on which to rest notes and place hands. The focus may also be diffused by using presentation aids such as posters or overhead transparencies so that the audience will use these as a major focal point. Handouts also divert the attention of members of the group, as they will be looking at these handouts as they are discussed, thus relieving the pressure on the speaker. Audience participation is also an excellent deterrent to feeling exposed. Pose problems, supervise exercises, conduct critiques, invite questions, and lead discussions. Allow the audience to help with the presentation.

DELIVERY OF THE SPEECH

Enthusiasm is a contagious emotion. The enthusiastic speaker manages to imbue an audience with it. Little can be more effective, perhaps, in sparking up a delivery than the obvious zest exhibited by the speaker. People respond more easily to emotional appeals than to rational appeals. If one believes earnestly in what one is saying and realizes its value, this enthusiasm shows in the voice, face, eyes, and gestures. Wave arms; lower voices; whisper; hiss; raise voices; shout! Let the eyes flash; grin; make faces; laugh; groan! Strike the lectern to add emphasis! Point excitedly to people! Write major points on a chalkboard. Ask demanding, challenging questions. Watch what happens when this is done. Watch the audience light up and come to life. They will return a speaker's grins, groans, laughs, and sighs.

Eye contact is one of the most important things to consider during delivery of a speech. Make eye contact with many people in the audience—with all of them, if possible, but only for a few minutes each. Singling people out for eye contact, one by one, not only assures them of the speaker's interest in addressing them directly but also helps the speaker judge how effectively he/she is coming across. It enables the speaker to know when the pace is lagging and when a topic or point of great interest has been touched on. It is the source of the speaker's feedback.

SPEAKING TO PERSUADE

Persuasion is the central objective and the ultimate aim of much public speaking. It operates most effectively in a positive atmosphere. Vocabulary, coupled with a lively imagination, is the key to personal persuasion. Verbal brushes paint indelible pictures on the human mind. Replace shapeless abstractions with concrete words that are vibrant and expressive. Use vigorous sentences that say what is meant instead of sluggish phrases that say nothing and go nowhere.

Learn the language of the listeners—every profession has its nomenclature, its own distinctive terms and language. Speak this language. This is a device that lends itself to persuasion. Listeners will appreciate the fact that the speaker thought enough of them to learn their language.

COMMUNICATING WITH THE BODY

Speak not with words alone. Let the language of the body help to persuade. Meet the audience with a smile. Replace the rigid jaw with a relaxed smile. Don't squirm impatiently while waiting for an introduction.

Posture is a basic part of body language. Employ good balance, stand erect with weight slightly forward. Appear positive; look active and ready to go. Don't be afraid to move—walk away from the lecturn, move into the audience. This helps remove an artificial barrier; it helps to hold attention. Upon leaving the lectern, move about with a purpose, but don't pace the room like a caged lion. Learn the language of children; their gestures are natural and communicative. Watch how a child talks with hands, shoulders, and eyes. The shoulders rise, the outstretched palms move upward; eyebrows are lifted, and the lower lip protrudes—"I don't know why I did it."

According to William Turner, "body language conveys 40 percent of your communication message. Here, then, are some rules for natural gestures: (1) Don't use the same gesture over and over again. (2) Don't gesture continuously. (3) Make your gestures fit the environment and the size of your audience. (4) Don't terminate a gesture at the halfway mark. Complete it. (5) The arms, shoulders, and face should work in concert to communicate and persuade. (6) Strive for naturalness. Don't let your gestures call attention to themselves."[1] Gestures usually reinforce thoughts.

DEVELOPMENT OF SPEAKING SKILLS

It is necessary to make students aware that communication is a two-way process. This involves sending the message and receiving the message. It is well to remember that the human communication process is always the same and does not change in formal speech, informal conversation, interviews, or business conferences. It does, however, require that the communicators at both ends adapt themselves to the specific situation and to each other.

The students need to realize the barriers to communication and how these barriers may be overcome. The largest barrier is the self-centered attitude. It must be stressed that the *you* attitude is an absolute for complete communication. Another barrier arises when there are differences in background and experiences—the meaning individual speakers are trying to convey may be interpreted differently by different listeners.

Still another barrier is resistance to change. The principle of least effort influences everyone. The listener in many instances may have a closed mind.

Yet another barrier is to refute rather than understand. It is necessary that students listen for the message rather than think about their reply. Another barrier might be that of age—the generation gap—the fact that words mean different things to different people. For example, in today's language among the young, the word *bad* really means something is terrific, *cool* means everything is running smoothly, and *hunk* means an extremely good-looking male.

As these several barriers to communication are lifted, students will become more outgoing, will improve academically, will be more contented with themselves, and will become more gracious individuals.

Probably the most glaring immediate problem currently facing educators is the poor grammar usage that prevails in the educational environment. This is a constant source of concern and needs to be addressed daily—on an individual basis and with entire classes. Not only is it necessary to study

---

[1]Turner, William. *Secrets of Personal Persuasion*. Englewood Cliffs, N.J.; Prentice-Hall, 1985. p. 95.

grammar units and have reviews in this area, but it is imperative that students use proper grammar when conversing—even to the point where the instructor may interrupt informal conversations to suggest certain changes in the spoken words.

The *I* attitude, or self-centered barrier, needs to be addressed daily. This relates to a positive/negative attitude. An example of this might be "I'm going for a drink" rather than "May I please get a drink?"

Students should appreciate the value of a dictionary and a thesaurus. Using these aids habitually will increase the students' vocabularies, thus improving their communication processes.

A unit of instruction on public speaking has tremendous advantages—especially if students are allowed to speak on exciting or interesting subjects. Their minds and imaginations will be actively engaged. This can be a truly exciting learning experience and, at the same time, can help to develop and strengthen the fundamentals of public speaking.

EVALUATION OF SPEAKING SKILLS

Evaluation of speaking skills must be by nature informal. Units and reviews of grammar can be evaluated by traditional methods such as the grading of papers in which the students have demonstrated their knowledge and by quizzing the students on parts of the unit and evaluating the quizzes.

Rather than have a unit where all students must prepare and deliver their speeches in the same frame of time, the instructor might, at the beginning of the year, wish to set up a schedule in which the students would complete their research and prepare their speeches while other units are being taught. This would create a change of pace for the students as the year passes. They would listen more closely and enjoy each other's efforts rather than become bored from listening to repetitious speeches daily.

Evaluation of public speaking can be done in several ways. One can evaluate the text while the student is composing it. One can also evaluate the execution of the speech at the time of its delivery. This would permit the student to have two grades for the same effort. Or, the instructor could choose to grade the content and presentation of the speech at the time of its delivery. Regardless of the grading procedure, students can do nothing but enhance their ability to communicate with others if they have put forth some effort in the development of a public speaking assignment.

CONCLUSION

The development of speaking skills and the development of personality reflect the growth of the student. In formal presentations the student needs to develop the speech, organize the speech, and shape the speech before even considering the presentation. Once this is accomplished, the presentation must be attacked. The delivery of the speech should include persuasion, emotion, the use of body language, and an awareness that communication is a two-way process. Having the student develop and present speeches is an assignment that can do nothing but enhance communication skills.

CHAPTER 4

Developing Basic Writing Skills

C. GLENN PEARCE

Virginia Commonwealth University, Richmond

Scot Dyer sat silently at his desk—pondering, worried. It was Monday morning, and he had just returned from his boss's office, where she had rejected a report he had submitted earlier for approval. "Scot," she had said, "you and I have worked together for a long time. I've no doubt that you researched this topic well. Nor have I any doubt that you are the right person to have completed the work; you know more about this subject than anyone in the department."

She had paused for a moment, and he had seen from the expression on her face that she had dreaded to press the issue. Yet, she had continued: "This report, though, does not reflect the quality of research you have done, nor does it demonstrate your extensive knowledge of the subject."

"What do you mean, Madelyn?" he had asked. "I spent four work days plus two weekends of my own time to get the job done on time. I've really worked hard on this project."

"Yes, Scot, I know you have," she had said reassuringly. "You're one of the most dedicated members of the department, and I think you know I have appreciated your hard work and dedication ever since you came to work here. Still the fact remains that the report itself is essentially unclear. Also, most of the major points are buried within the text, making them appear minor even when they are clearly stated. Spelling, punctuation, and syntax errors abound as well. As much as I would like to approve the report, I cannot. These errors must be corrected before we send it forward for the vice-president's approval."

After a long pause, Scot had finally said, "When do you want it?"

"Tomorrow."

"Tomorrow!"

"Yes. The board meets Friday, and Mr. Workel (the vice-president) will need at least two days to study the report before presenting it to the board members. Because we have so little time left, I took time to mark the problem areas and made several suggestions about organization. That is not something I can do regularly, however."

"Okay," he had said, looking dejected. "Somehow, I'll get it done." Then as he had arisen to leave, Madelyn had said, "Remember, Scot—tomorrow."

Scenarios like that involving Scot Dyer take place daily in American businesses—by the thousands. Study after study done year after year reveals that business practitioners in general are regarded as poor writers (and poor speakers, too). Those of us who work to help our business students become better writers never seriously refute the results of these studies. We know from experience that they are accurate for the most part.

What then are our choices? Are we to leave business to train its own writers, for example? No, the business setting, while a good place to review and improve writing skills, is a poor place to develop *basic* writing skills. Nor could we expect students to develop these skills on their own. A skill is best developed under the guidance of a trained supervisor, an instructor in this case. The classroom then is probably the best, most opportune setting for developing basic writing skills.

Given the classroom as the setting, the question remains how to go about developing these critical skills. That is the topic for discussion in this chapter—how to build and evaluate basic writing skills in the business education curriculum.

BUILDING BASIC WRITING SKILLS

As we read the literature on business writing, about which there is a great body of work, we see three issues that cause confusion. One is that of the document itself. Which business documents will students be writing? Here, the discussion is limited to letters, memorandums, and reports, the most commonly written business documents.

Another issue is subject matter—exactly what topics are to be taught? So, to avoid confusion, the following commonly taught topics are included:

1. The principles of style and tone—clarity, courtesy, conciseness, and so forth
2. Grammar, including spelling, punctuation, capitalizations, and syntax
3. Audience analysis, including how different types of messages are likely to affect receivers—sometimes called the psychology of writing
4. Organization—from sentence construction to that of the entire document.

The third issue is semantics. What do you mean when you say *approach, method,* or *technique*? So, let's call an *approach* a general way to organize classroom instruction, a *method* a general way to organize both students and subject matter for instruction, and a *technique* a specific way of teaching skills.

To clarify, assume that an example of an approach is to teach business writing as a specific subject in a self-contained classroom. An example of a method is group instruction; and an example of a technique is to lecture students about the subject matter.

Approaches. Two popular general approaches to teaching business writing in the classroom setting are *discrete* and *integrated*. You take a discrete approach when you teach an independent, separate course in the subject and an integrated approach when you teach writing as part of a course in another area—office management, for instance.

Generally, a discrete course is designed to direct the primary effort in the class toward building the basic writing skills. In such classes the topics students work with will be business or business related, but the topics themselves take on secondary emphasis. That is, your main goal in such a course is to teach principles, grammar, audience analysis, and organization. While students always do learn a great deal about the topics they write about in a discrete course, they understand their main objective is to build writing skills. Therefore, topical learning may occur incidentally but is not the focus of the course. Whether students write from prior knowledge, do research, or do some combination of the two, please note that knowledge of subject matter is necessary for effective skill building. Clarity of expression is enhanced, for example, in direct relation to the extent of knowledge of the topic. You can see this effect at work in all applications of the principles of effective writing, but the same is not true for grammar, audience analysis, or organization. Topical knowledge is not as closely related to growth in these areas, even though it can be argued persuasively that a relationship exists. It's just a matter of degree.

An integrated approach to teaching business writing may be the only way you teach writing skills, or it may be something you do in addition to instruction in a discrete course. There seems to be little argument about the merits of such an approach, just as there seems little argument about the need for instruction in discrete courses. At this time the integrated approach is very popular in graduate business education courses but is less popular in undergraduate courses. Sometimes called "writing across the curriculum," integrated instruction has its advantages and disadvantages.

Some of the advantages of integrated instruction are that students are (1) usually more knowledgeable about the topics they write about, (2) more careful than usual about how they write because they know writing performance is part of the course requirements, and (3) able to get feedback about their writing performance they may not normally get. In addition, integrated instruction puts writing in a more realistic setting than does discrete instruction, thereby generating more interest in improvement. Also, it can be a more efficient way to teach—some say review—these skills, from both a time and cost-effectiveness perspective.

Some of the disadvantages of this type of instruction are that students (1) may not take writing skill development as seriously as they might in a discrete course and (2) may not have enough time to devote to serious skill building. Too, whenever the writing instructor is also the course content instructor, the "instructor variable" is more pronounced. For instance, a course content instructor in an office management course may or may not be a proficient instructor in business writing skills. In addition, the content instructor may place more or less emphasis on the writing skills aspects of the course.

Should you ponder the matter, you would add to this list of the advantages and disadvantages of integrated instruction; and it would be helpful for us to share these discoveries. Yet, to look at general approaches to building writing skills is to take a very broad view. Once that decision has been made, though, you can do much more specific planning.

Methods. Using the earlier definition of methods for teaching basic writing skills, both students and subject matter are involved. As for students, you may organize them into groups or teach them individually. Student groups may be as large as a full class or as small as two or three people. Sometimes, a combination of large/small-group instruction is used. For example, an instructor may teach a class of 20, 30, or 150 students in a single room and then use breakout sections for working on problems and cases. In such an instance, more than one instructor will be required for breakouts if the whole group instruction involves a large number of students; or breakouts may be scheduled at different times of the day or week if only one instructor is available. In fact, breakout sections are ideal for group instruction in basic writing skills regardless of class size.

In individual instruction, one instructor teaches one student and may conduct sessions as tutoring or through criticizing assignments. Even though individual instruction is expensive as such in the classroom setting, much individual help can be given. For example, students can help one another, a method that works especially well when the more talented or experienced students help those who are less able. Another example is for the teacher to work with individuals while other class members work on other assignments. Both these examples will work for individual instruction outside the classroom as well as inside. Using any or all of these types of individual instruction will result in better feedback for individuals about their work. That seems desirable considering that almost all writing on the job, including collaborative writing, is done individually. Rarely will two or more people sit together trying to agree on which words to write on paper or computer; it's just too time-consuming and, therefore, too expensive to work that way.

Unlike the methods used to organize students, those used to organize subject matter are numerous. The most popular ones involve using textbooks, simulations, study guides, cases, and readings. While these methods are quite often used in some combination with one another, most instructors use a commercial textbook or some other type of text material as the basic organizational device. Some instructors teach directly from the text, which usually includes exercises too. Others teach from their experience and use materials they have gathered or devised for in-class examples and as handouts; but many of these instructors still require that students have textbooks for study or reference.

An instructor can do an effective job without the convenience of a textbook, though. In fact, realism is so important to the experience of learning to write well that any textbook-based instruction will be greatly improved when supplemented with some type of instruction from the world of work. One method for making the classroom-based writing experience more realistic is to use a simulation. Generally speaking, simulations are of two types: in-basket and work-flow, both of which require the student to "take a job" in a company and perform the various writing activities the job calls for. With an in-basket simulation the student performs a series of isolated writing activities. In contrast, a work-flow simulation calls for routing work from job to job, providing students with the opportunity to work with other people's writing in some way or to use others' writing as a basis for performing the next writing task. While the work-flow simulation is much more difficult to manage in the classroom environment, it does offer a broader range of learning experiences. Both types of simulations offer about as much realism as a student can get without actually going to work for a firm.

A simulation may be published in print form, on a computer disk, or in print form with an accompanying computer disk. Please note that a simulation is not necessarily limited to supplemental status. Some instructors who do not use a textbook may use a simulation as the main method of organizing instruction. In such cases the course content material will have to be provided in some other way because simulations normally do not contain that type of material.

Study guides are most often used to review and reinforce the instructional material students learn in the classroom. Thus, a study guide is almost always used as a supplement in business writing courses. The extent to which this type of material is needed depends on the students' capabilities. Unless students are grouped by ability when assigned to a particular section of a course, some students may need the additional help a study guide offers. For this reason many instructors either leave the choice to the student or suggest that certain students use one once the need becomes apparent. Because most study guides accompany specific textbooks, the choice of the text forces the choice of the study guide—that is, unless the instructor chooses to provide the material on handouts or in some other form.

The case method is another popular way to teach business writing skills. Cases may be short or long, simple or complex, and primary or supplemental. Further, some cases are multidimensional in that they involve writing activities with research and oral presentations, for example. While cases are more popular as supplemental devices to text application, effective instruction can be given using the case method as the primary organizer. Those instructors who use the case method in this way most often integrate course content instruction into classroom activities as the course progresses. By doing this, they can assign cases on the first day of class if they wish.

Finally, readings—articles and essays about business writing—are widely used in teaching business writing skills. Although this may seem surprising given that readings appear distant from writing practice itself, the flexibility with which readings can be used may also be surprising. The following are examples of their use:

1. Preparation for discussion of the subject matter
2. Source for review and reinforcement of the subject matter
3. Exposure to different points of view about the subject matter
4. Basis for assigning various writing projects.

Assigning readings, then, can be a valuable asset in helping students become better business writers. You can find excellent readings in commercial books, professional journals, newspapers, and business magazines. Most often, business writing instructors use readings to supplement the course content in some way rather than to depend on them as the main method.

Techniques. Techniques—specific ways to help students develop their writing skills—are too sundry to attempt an exhaustive discussion of them in a single chapter such as this one. A better approach may be to identify and discuss some of the more popular ones. Seven of these popular techniques are lecture/discussion, guest speakers, research, critiques, process, computer writing, and time pressure. Basic to the effective use of these techniques is application, the assumption that students learn to write by writing and that they will be required to write as much as circumstances will allow.

The lecture/discussion technique is still the most popular single way instructors expose students to appropriate business writing practices. The instructors present the points for consideration and discuss them with their students. The interaction between instructor and students brings this technique to life; students get more from these sessions when they are talked with rather than talked to. The opportunity to interact generates interest in the subject matter and makes students more attentive and more willing to share their ideas.

Using guest speakers works well in teaching writing skills. You can use this technique to generate interest through diversified presentation and to bring more realism to the classroom setting. The best guest speakers are business practitioners and other instructors. The practitioner, a person who writes daily as a part of his or her job, can share the world-of-work experience with students to give them ideas about what they will have to do when they go to work. Such a person may work for a local company or in many instances may be members of the class you are teaching. Practitioners can underscore areas of agreement and disagreement between what is taught in writing courses and what is practiced on the job.

The instructors you invite to speak to your students may teach business writing themselves, or they may teach other business content courses, finance or marketing, for example. On the one hand, the writing instructor you invite may bring a different point of view to the subject matter, emphasize areas you have not discussed, and interact with students in a way that may not be natural for you. On the other hand, instructors of other content courses can discuss the importance of developing various writing abilities in the areas in which they teach. Too, this type of instructor can discuss the various writing assignments students must be able to do when they take courses in that person's subject area and in jobs in that field.

Asking students to conduct field or library research is another popular technique used by business writing instructors. Field research may involve telephone or personal interviews with business practitioners to learn what they write on the job and how they go about it. Library research is entirely different from that done in the field. In one way it is less effective given that this type of research is secondary and, therefore, may be more conceptual than experiential. In another way it may be more effective in that it is possible to acquire a wider range of information in less time. Further, gathering information in the library gives students greater control in selecting the information itself—that is, if instructors allow their students to participate in the selection process.

The critique as a technique is a powerful learning device. Through the feedback process a critique offers, students can learn a lot about how the messages they write are perceived by others. These outside critiques may be given by fellow students or by the instructor. In combination with self-criticism—students' critiques of their own work—critiques by others can help students improve their writing skills dramatically in a short time. Just as students can critique writing done by themselves and other class members, they can gather real letters, memos, and reports from company files and criticize these documents according to the information they learn in the classroom about good writing skills.

The next writing technique, process, has been used extensively in basic composition classes for several years but is just now becoming popular among business writing instructors. Instructors who employ the process technique operate on the assumption that writing is a process, not a discrete act, and that good writing requires careful planning, editing, and revision. As a result, students are asked to prepare a first draft of a document and then rewrite it one or more times based on self-examination or feedback they are given. A clear disadvantage of the process technique is that it is time-consuming, both for the instructor and the student. A great advantage, of course, is that the final draft is likely to be greatly improved over the first one.

Computer writing is already extremely popular among business writing instructors and is likely to continue to grow in popularity. Computers have become the "writing tool" of choice. Instructors who have access to the necessary hardware and software very often take full advantage of the opportunity. That computer writing is more efficient than other comparable techniques is indisputable. Students can prepare the original draft and revise and edit their work much more easily using the computer. Not only that, more and more companies have automated their offices, and therefore using the computer to write business documents is the type of experience students will have once they go to work. To gain this type of experience in the classroom setting helps ease the transition from school to job.

The primary disadvantages to requiring that students write their assignments on the computer are that (1) some students can't keyboard by touch, which slows them down considerably, and (2) some students may never have used a word processing program, and thus at least some classroom time may have to be spent teaching them to do this.

Finally, some instructors ask students to write at least some assignments under time pressure. Because writing on the job more often than not requires the ability to write rapidly, some instructors believe the classroom is a good place to begin. Using this technique requires in-class writing in order to control the time factor. Should you choose to use this technique, a good way to proceed is to allow more time in the beginning than you do later on. For example, you may allow 30 minutes to write a letter or memo the first time or two and then reduce the time to 25 minutes, 20 minutes, and so forth as students develop skill. Remember, though, as you employ this technique that the complexity of the writing task and the length of the document must be taken into account when you decide on the time limit.

As instructors employ the appropriate approaches, methods, and techniques in teaching basic business writing skills, the students must be evaluated to determine the extent of progress they are making.

EVALUATING BASIC WRITING SKILLS

Any evaluation system would benefit from a *pretest* given on knowledge of grammar and basic writing skills. Because both types of knowledge are needed to develop proficiency levels needed in business, an instructor needs to know what levels students bring to class at the beginning. A pretest can establish these levels for each student, thus serving as an excellent diagnostic device. Pretests can be used to determine which aspects of the course to emphasize and which students need specific types of help.

A *posttest* makes a nice complement to a pretest in that an instructor can use it to evaluate progress made during a time period or at the end of the course. Together, pretests and posttests are useful in saving time and challenging students appropriately.

Behind the development of a complete evaluation system that might include pretesting and posttesting are three basic assumptions. The first one involves the idea of *judgment.* Just as any evaluation is a judgment, a judgment is subjective in nature. Nevertheless, the need to measure progress dictates that some type of evaluation system be used.

The second assumption involves *motivation,* the need to devise an evaluation system that will motivate students to improve their writing skills. While motivation may be negative or positive, most instructors believe positive motivation works better. Because different evaluation systems work differently depending on instructors' choices and their students' abilities, most instructors work out systems by trial and error. Experience, then, complemented by study becomes the most common determinant of how best to motivate students through evaluation.

The third assumption involves *objectives.* Students need to know at the outset what levels of performance are expected of them and how that performance will be measured. Effective objectives must be based on standards, which must be set before objectives can be established. In setting standards, instructors should determine the factors for consideration—that is, what will be evaluated and how. Once these factors are set, they can devise their grading systems.

Setting standards. A standard is a predetermined level of performance either set by the instructor, perhaps in consultation with other instructors, or taken from some authoritative source. While standards may be set in various ways, writing instructors currently use one or more of the following bases:

1. Actual or perceived minimal performance levels in business or in the institution where the course is taught
2. Group competition, in which individual performance is compared to that of the group
3. Self-competition, in which individual performance is compared to the past performance of the same individual.

Writing instructors have various opinions about which base or mix of bases is most appropriate. Many believe that the use of minimal performance levels in business is the best standard, for example. Yet, those who wish to use this standard as the base find it difficult to determine just what those levels are and whether they differ from company to company or industry to industry, for instance.

Factors for consideration. Because instructors evaluate how well their students' writing conforms to the subject matter, this discussion takes us back to the earlier one on topics. In that discussion, these topics were given as (1) the principles of style and tone, (2) grammar, (3) audience analysis, and (4) organization. In addition to these factors, many instructors evaluate the quality of the ideas or content. Should you include content in the measure, be sure to judge whether the presentation is thorough and current and whether it is based on sound reasoning.

Grading systems. For the most part, general grading systems are dictated by institutions in which instructors work; they provide frameworks within which to operate. The most common of these systems are letter grade, point, and pass/fail.

Letter grades of A, B, C, D, or F can be assigned on students' papers, for one assignment or for an entire course. Generally, instructors comment on papers and assign grades that represent the quality of the work.

With point system, the instructor will deduct specific points for individual violations of the subject matter. For example, three points may be deducted for a wordy expression or a comma error. The most common of these systems are based on 10- or 7-point spreads that then can be converted to letter grades if desired.

When you grade on a pass/fail basis, you make only one judgment. The student either passes or fails an assignment or the course itself. Pass/fail grading is more popular for noncredit courses and seminars than for credit courses. In addition, this system is quite popular for screening examinations when instructors are determining who should be required to take a course in business writing. These examinations are more widely used in graduate than in undergraduate education. (Please note that screening examinations differ from pretests, which were discussed earlier.)

CONCLUSION

Courses in basic writing skills have become very popular in business education programs today, either as separate courses or as part of more general courses in business communication. There seems to be a consensus among business educators that all or most students, especially undergraduates, need to improve their writing skills before going to work. This proliferation of instruction in basic writing skills does not guarantee us proficient writers, of course, but it does guarantee that students will be more proficient than if they had not taken such a course. While the future looks bright, we need to devote our energies to improving the quality of instruction in this critical part of the business communication curriculum. The information provided in this chapter may help in some small way as we reach toward that goal.

As we continue to improve instruction in basic business writing skills, we will build on the trend toward graduating fewer Scot Dyers.

CHAPTER 5

Developing Basic Reading Skills

JOAN SLIVA BRIGGAMAN
Connecticut State Department of Education, Hartford

JANICE M. SLIVA
Smithtown Central School District, Smithtown, New York

Reading is a skill that most people possess from the second they are born. From early nonverbal reading, such as eye contact and voice recognition between parent and child, to high-level skills that bring meaning to the printed word, reading is communication. This chapter on developing basic reading skills is divided into two major sections. The first section will provide readers with an overview of what reading is. The second section will explain how business educators can develop their students' reading skills.

UNDERSTANDING READING

Reading is not an isolated skill; it is a process. In order to read in the most conventional sense, a person must be able to interact with print, to understand the author's meaning and purpose, and to apply what has been read.

Learning to read. At the earliest level of formal reading, the time when students are learning to read, there are several interpretations as to exactly what constitutes reading. Among the interpretations are those from the phonics, whole word, speaking or listening, and comprehension perspectives. Learning styles are also important to consider when learning to read.

PHONICS. One of the more familiar methods of teaching reading is phonics, whereby students are taught to put sounds to the symbols called letters. When the sound of each letter has been learned, students are taught how to blend these sounds together to make words. The ability to decipher these sounds into words is called decoding. While decoding is an integral skill in reading, it in and of itself does not constitute reading. Taught in isolation, decoding fails to include comprehension of words.

WHOLE WORD. Another method of teaching students to read is the whole-word approach. This method of teaching reading is one in which the whole word to be learned is presented to students, and they in effect memorize the word. In some ways, this method is similar to learning math facts by heart. Often there is little understanding associated with the words being learned, and students cannot transfer word meanings to other situations.

SPEAKING/LISTENING. Before reading can be meaningful, students must have the ability to manipulate language through speaking and listening. These are experiences that beginning readers bring from home. They hear language in daily conversations and through books read to them, and they question constantly. These skills are prerequisites that aid children in developing comprehension.

COMPREHENSION. There must always be comprehension, meaning associated with the words that are being learned. Meanings associated with even the most simple words are the beginnings of comprehension. Initially learning the meanings of words can be called vocabulary development. As students' reading word banks increase, the words are strung together to form simple sentences.

Comprehension occurs when students are able to read text and answer questions about the written material. Initial sentences are short in length and simple in construction; as students increase their ability to read, the sentence construction becomes more complex. One of the greatest differences between early learning and advanced learning is in the complexity of the length and the syntax of the material being read.

LEARNING STYLES. Why is it that all students do not read with ease, learn at the same rate, or understand the teacher's presentation? The answers are not simple. Just as all teachers have different styles of teaching, so too, do all students have different styles of learning.

Extensive research has been done on learning styles. Some of the research points out that many students fail not because they are disinterested on lazy but rather because the manner in which the instruction was presented did not match their learning styles.

Educators need to be aware of the fact that some students are auditory learners and find lecture presentations very effective; other students are visual learners and find presentations with visual aids or independent reading assignments crucial to their academic success. There are other students who need to be active participants in lessons to gain full meaning from the instruction. The purpose of being aware of learning styles is not that educators should teach each of their lessons five times but rather that their teaching should incorporate a variety of styles, such as a lecture that uses visual aids and study guides, to assist learners in focusing attention on the expected learning.

Reading to learn. Once students have learned the essentials of reading, they are ready to apply these skills seriously in order to learn from reading. While most students learn to read, many have difficulty in transferring these skills to the content materials they are expected to use. An issue in content-area reading instruction is how to instruct students so that they are best able to study and learn from the information presented in the printed materials they use each day.

Earlier in this article the viewpoint was presented that teaching skills in isolation may enable students to acquire skills and yet to be unable to transfer them to other situations. The same premise is suggested in teaching reading skills in content areas. It is important to understand that at various times in reading experiences, people read for different purposes. People read for pleasure, to learn how to do something, and to gain specific information. Each of these circumstances requires different skills and points of reference. There are few, if any, people who have not faced reading a textbook for a course and bemoaned the fact that they can read a current best seller in two days and then take a week to read two 30-page chapters of a particular textbook. This is precisely what happens when people read to learn, and it is the difficulty that students who are capable readers face as they suddenly discover that they are reading but not understanding. It is precisely the reason why teachers need to teach specific reading techniques and skills in content classes to ensure content learning.

Readiness to read. When reading readiness is mentioned, the usual reaction is to think about activities that are presented to young children prior to formal reading instruction. Generally readiness refers to the skill of students at a given age to respond adequately to the requirements of a task. Readiness always impacts the effectiveness of the learning process. Teachers ensure students' readiness through preparatory activities such as setting purposes for reading, building backgrounds and experiences, and teaching unfamiliar vocabulary. These steps should be applied at all grade levels and in all content areas. Activities developed and presented that include these steps assist in providing a structure that helps learners build bridges between what they know and what they will study.

Teachers can structure their instruction so that both content and reading can be taught. The framework for doing this includes cognitive readiness and motivation, background information and review, anticipation and purpose, direction, and language development. These aspects are the elements of effective teaching.

Selection of instructional materials. Instructional materials used by content-area teachers to provide instruction are learning devices and not just sources of information to be presented to learners. The selected instructional materials should present information that will aid students in achieving the learning objectives their teachers wish them to learn. While readability is one important criterion, there are at least four other items to be considered when selecting appropriate instructional materials. These include concept load, background information, format and style, and organization.

READABILITY. Readability is determined through the use of formulas. These formulas usually use varying combinations of length of sentence and difficulty of vocabulary to determine the reading difficulty of material. One problem that impacts the readability level of textbooks is the specialized vocabulary, which tends to inflate the readability level. Some formulas include the complexity of sentences in calculating the reading difficulty. Not all formulas are appropriate for all grade levels. A caution in using readability formulas exclusively is that when different formulas, such as the Fry, Dale-Chall, Flesch, and SMOG formulas, are applied to the same materials, often different readability levels result. What readability formulas do provide is a quick estimate of the reading difficulty of materials being reviewed by evaluators.

CONCEPT LOAD. Concept load is established by evaluators actually counting the number of concepts being introduced and assessing how abstract they are. From approximately age 11, students begin to build and manipulate abstract ideas without reference to concrete examples. The ability of students to assimilate conceptual ideas varies; therefore, the concept load presented in textbooks they are asked to read must be addressed.

BACKGROUND INFORMATION. Background information is an idea presented previously. Just as it is used to prepare students to attain instructional objectives, it is closely aligned to concept load in determining the reading difficulty of the materials used for instruction. Many of the materials assume that students have previous experiences that will assist them in using the materials. Here, too, evaluators will have to determine whether the students have sufficient background to enable them to learn from the new material being presented.

FORMAT AND STYLE. Format and style are also key considerations in determining reading difficulty. Students will read material that is attractively presented more successfully than solid text. The tenor of the material or the author's style will also affect the reading difficulty of the material. Additional consideration should be given to inclusion of graphics, pictures, maps, glossaries, and appendixes, all of which assist students' learning. Materials should also be reviewed to assess whether such aids are located appropriately within the text where they are needed for optimum learner assistance.

ORGANIZATION. Organization of content is crucial in selecting appropriate instructional materials. It is important that concepts are presented in sequential order. Ideas that lead logically from one to the next will also assist learners in gaining understanding from the materials.

In addition to the criteria suggested, additional criteria may be needed in specific learning situations and content areas. No one of these criteria alone is sufficient to determine the suitability of instructional materials; but when used together, they can present a meaningful view of instructional materials and assist content-area teachers in selecting appropriate instructional materials for their students.

Services of reading consultants. Teachers can help the students in their classes by using the resources available in their school systems. Most schools have reading consultants. These people have been specially trained not only to work with students who have difficulty in reading but also to share with subject-area teachers their knowledge of a variety of instructional techniques that will assist the teachers in developing teaching strategies so that all students—not just those with reading difficulties—can improve their reading skills.

Reading consultants can serve as resource persons when new instructional materials are being selected. They can assist in the development of appropriate criteria for evaluating and adopting content materials. Once the content materials have been selected, reading consultants can make suggestions to tailor materials to students' individual needs. Reading consultants can also help by assessing whether other instructional materials can be useful, by developing model lessons, and by suggesting changes in presentations or techniques to meet instructional goals. Furthermore, reading consultants can design workshops to help integrate special skills into content-area instruction.

Reading consultants can also assist in analyses of tests. Many times students fail tests because of the wording used in test items. Reading consultants can ensure that test questions ask what teachers are attempting to ascertain.

DEVELOPING READING SKILLS

After business educators understand basic reading-related concepts, they are ready to ensure student learning by incorporating reading instruction into business education content materials.

Ensuring learning. What can business educators do to increase students' content-area learning and to improve their reading skills? The following four steps are a way of assisting teachers in ensuring learning in both areas.

First, business educators need to identify those learning objectives that they consider important for their students to master in the specific content area. Second, once business educators have identified those specific content learning objectives, they should identify those specific reading and studying skills that their students will need in order to attain the selected objectives. In other words, the objectives drive the skills. Third, after selecting the objectives and the specific reading skills needed for achievement, business educators need to assess which skills the students already have and which ones need to be taught. This analysis of students' skills can be accomplished through informal testing that teachers then use in planning their courses of instruction. Such informal assessments can be prepared with the assistance of reading consultants. Fourth, business educators should select the appropriate skills to match the subject instruction. All of the reading-related skills are not taught at once. The teaching of such skills should be purposeful and functional. The purpose of these steps and the related instruction is to provide students with the necessary specific reading and studying skills so that they can achieve the content-area learning goals their teachers have selected.

All teachers have a common goal: to provide their students with the best possible education in order to enable them to achieve their potentials and to become productive members of society. By understanding the relationship between teaching styles and students' learning styles, educators will be better teachers, and their students will learn subject matter with a higher degree of mastery. While it would be wonderful if schools could match each individual student's and teacher's styles, in most cases this is not practical. What can be done, however, is to provide teachers with a variety of strategies and approaches to use to make students better learners.

Teaching reading skills. An important goal of business education is to prepare individuals for work, and students enter business education programs expecting instruction in skills that will prepare them for work. In order to satisfy these goals, business educators must know how much reading is necessary, what kinds of literature must be read, and what skills are required to attain, maintain, and achieve upward mobility in employment or lateral transferability across employment clusters. This means that a high priority for reading in business education must be the development of the ability to read for occupational competency. Business teachers can develop students' reading skills by using prerequisites for reading, by understanding the responsibilities of learning, by overcoming challenges to learning, by understanding the characteristics of reading materials, by teaching reading to understand, by teaching reading to think, by teaching reading to proof, and by considering reading aspects of testing.

PREREQUISITES FOR LEARNING. If the goal or outcome of the business education program is to ensure that students enrolled in the program can read the literature required to enter and survive in a business-related occupation, then establishing the reading levels of those materials and of the students entering the program and then considering those levels during instruction is one means of ensuring student success in the program and in the workplace. After all, studies of correspondence from 15 different business areas have determined that the writing levels of the correspondence are at a higher reading level than that of the average U.S. citizen.

When reading skills are prerequisites to enter into a business program, they should be used as the basis for decisions that provide remedial assistance as required on an individual basis using business materials and skill enhancement through appropriate business instruction. The whole purpose of this is to bring all students to the level needed to prepare them for work. A reading prerequisite can aid potential dropouts and/or underachievers, as well as enhance the skills of all students. Assessment of students' abilities can be accomplished through a variety of sources that include standardized tests, informal reading tests, teachers' observations, anecdotal records, and students' self-evaluations.

RESPONSIBILITIES OF LEARNING. A list of employability skills for business students usually includes such things as the ability to keyboard, to format documents, to proofread, to answer the telephone, to take messages, to use business machines, and others. These are important skills, but the list is incomplete without listing these additional skills: the ability to use technical vocabulary; the ability to recognize context clues, key words, main ideas, and detail; the ability to recall information and to separate fact from opinion; the ability to follow directions, to sequence steps, and to ask questions; and the ability to interpret information, to predict outcomes, and to draw conclusions. The curriculum and lesson plans for every business course should give attention to all of these skills and knowledges as well as specific business subject matter.

All business teachers want their students to do the required reading so that they will learn the subject matter and be active participants in the classroom. If business teachers will take the time to follow the suggestions given in this article, they will help their students to develop more positive attitudes toward learning and reading.

Business teachers ought to know the reading levels of assigned textbooks and supplementary reading materials, know the reading levels of their students, and know the reading levels of the occupational literature. They should take the time to prepare students for reading the assigned materials; to show students how to preview the reading materials; to provide supplementary reading materials and aids; to show students how to learn and use the technical vocabulary; to show students how to read at various rates based on the material and purpose for reading; and to provide students with opportunities to "try out" test questions and problems.

CHALLENGES TO OVERCOME. Along with responsibilities come challenges. While business teachers do not have to be convinced that their students need help, often business teachers are frustrated by conditions beyond their control including a wide range of student abilities in the same class; large pupil-teacher ratios; lack of time to teach reading and subject matter; lack of training and confidence in the teaching of reading; no funds for tutors, teacher aides, or reading consultants; school reading programs that are narrow in scope; and unwillingness on the part of students to accept the need for help in reading. As with all challenges, they can be overcome; to do so requires innovative approaches by business teachers and administrators.

CHARACTERISTICS OF READING MATERIALS. The reading materials that are used in business education classes also present some potential challenges that can be overcome. In order to develop reading skills in their classrooms, business educators must also understand the characteristics of reading materials. How many times have you heard the expression "This manual wasn't written by an educator"? What that person is really saying is that the reading level of the material is above his or her comprehension level and in many cases above that of the teacher as well. Recent studies have shown that there are wide differences in reading levels of textbooks written for the same audience as well as for different audiences. The same results were found when studying the software manuals that have become so vital to business education programs today.

Most textbook publishers, having taken great care to be certain that the reading levels of their instructional materials are appropriate for the needs of students at various ages, grades, and reading levels, will share information about the reading levels of their textbooks with business teachers. However, the same is not true of most publishers of software manuals that accompany databases, spreadsheets, and the like.

Once specific data has been gathered for the selected instructional materials in terms of such factors as readability, concept load, background information, format and style, and organization, business teachers can develop a set of strategies that will allow the use of materials of a higher level by students who are not functioning at that level. Useful strategies include overviews, information sheets, and self-checks.

Taking time to overview more difficult material by pointing out major concepts students should master; by explaining key terms, diagrams, illustrations, and charts; and by linking written material to classroom instruction will ensure that students are more comfortable with the more difficult material they will now read. Information sheets that guide students through the reading assignment by providing explanations at difficult points will also help students master the material. The most useful technique is the self-check. While most textbooks provide questions at the end of the chapter to reinforce students' learning, a better approach is to have a question or two at the end of each section of the reading material to provide students with the opportunity to self-check what they have learned before they get frustrated and stop reading. Teachers should prepare these questions when planning reading assignments and give them to the students as part of the overview. These same questions can then be used as discussion points the next day.

Reading is required in all business education courses—skill and nonskill courses—and all business teachers must pay attention to reading skills if they expect their students to be successful. Textbooks used in skill courses are similar to "how-to" manuals that require the ability to read and follow directions or illustrations accurately. Students will respond best when there is an orderly process from step to step and when directions build on each other and are clearly stated. Additional reinforcement through self-checks and information sheets to build mastery should include filling in the blanks around the concept to be learned, sequencing directions, and using sequential directions to complete rough drafts based on the concept.

Textbooks used in nonskill courses require students to glean main ideas. The relationship between students' reading levels and textbook reading levels influences the success of students in understanding main and supporting ideas. Mastery of these textbooks will depend on teachers' using strategies that will fit the individual differences of students—some students will need self-checks, some will need overviews, and some will need outlining techniques and assistance in preparing for tests.

READING TO UNDERSTAND. Students will be able to learn while reading if they are taught systematic approaches to studying textbooks and to taking notes. The SQ3R—survey, question, read, recite, and review—approach for reading and studying is one useful five-step method that business educators can teach their students.

Survey, the first step, uses the preview technique and provides familiarity with the author's format. It also draws upon background experiences for information that may be pertinent to the topic. When surveying, students should be taught to look for the following items: new vocabulary or important concepts highlighted by the use of boldface print and/or italics and paragraph headings or sections of the text presented in question or statement form. Students should also preview the questions at the end of the reading assignment before beginning the reading assignment. Textbooks with intermediate self-checks are excellent because students can preview these questions easily.

Question, the second step, sets a purpose for reading by using the paragraph headings or section titles as questions. Students should be trained to question the material they will read by using descriptive questions such as "What is it like?" or "What kind of situation is it" and comparative questions such as "How are two or more things different or alike?"

Read, the third step, is accomplished by reading the textbook assignment to answer the formulated questions. This technique gives a purpose for reading and allows location of the main ideas and the supporting details.

Recite, the fourth step, is answering the questions or summarizing what was read. Answers can be written or recited orally. This step helps the students check their mastery of what was read.

Review, the fifth step, has students reread those parts of the assignment that contain the information needed to answer questions, to find main ideas, and to master the subject area.

Students must also be taught a method to take notes or they will not be able to get meaningful learning from the experience. 5-R—record, reduce, recite, reflect, and review—note-taking is one useful method business educators can teach.

Prior to 5-R note-taking, divide an 8½- by 11-inch lined notebook page as follows: Draw a horizontal line across the page 2 inches from the bottom of the page. Draw a vertical line 2½ inches from the left edge of the paper beginning at the top of the page and extending downward to the 2-inch bottom line. There are now three sections on the page.

Record, the first step, uses the 6- by 9-inch section of the paper. On this section record as many meaningful facts and ideas as possible during the lecture.

Reduce, the second step, is accomplished by concisely summarizing the facts and ideas as soon as possible after the presentation in the 2½-inch column on the left side of the page.

Recite, the third step, is covering the 6- by 9-inch section and using the summary clues in the 2½-inch column to recite the detailed facts and ideas as fully as possible.

Reflect, the fourth step, requires reflecting on the new material in light of what is already known and recording the reflections on the bottom 2 inches of the page.

Review, the fifth step, is repeating steps three and four, recite and reflect, every week to ensure retention and application of what was learned.

The time spent teaching students to be efficient readers and learners with SQ3R and teaching them to be effective note-takers with 5-R note-taking will be repaid over and over.

READING TO THINK. Recent national reports have criticized educators for not teaching the higher-order skills such as decision making and problem solving or critical thinking. Business educators have perfect opportunities to be in the forefront of teaching and reinforcing these skills through case studies, practice sets, and simulations. At the same time business educators are building the comprehension abilities of their students. The only fault lies in the fact that business teachers fail to tell their students that they are making decisions and solving problems. Consequently, when students are asked to find answers in the business world, they say they can't because no one ever told them that they can.

Developing critical thinking takes time and requires learners to integrate a variety of skills. These skills include understanding the problem or situation, thinking about or internalizing the problem or situation, questioning, discussing, relating other relevant experiences, listing possible solutions and weighing advantages and disadvantages, selecting the best response, defending the selection, and implementing the selection. Computerized simulations are one option that business educators have for developing such decision-making and problem-solving skills.

READING TO PROOF. The ability to proofread is a number one priority for both business educators and the business community. The reading skills that underlie the ability to proofread include configuration of words, syllabication of words, word recognition skills, spelling skills, vocabulary mastery, and reading and understanding copy.

Mastery of proofreading skills and success in applying them require ample opportunities for practice and positive feedback. Computer software will play a larger part in proofreading, with packages already available to verify spelling, punctuation, grammar, and sentence structure. The use of this software will move proofreading from a tedious process into a decision-making opportunity.

READING AS PART OF TESTING. Business teachers must design tests that will complement the various learning styles and testing styles of their students. Some business educators argue that tests should be developed before the instruction takes place, and all instruction should center around the tests. This will occur naturally if business teachers have clear goals, teach to those goals, and then test based on those goals. A key component is to provide sample questions and desired answers so that students understand what is expected from them. In addition, business teachers should use a variety of types of testing formats, such as multiple choice, true/false, yes/no, fill in the blank, short answer, simulation, and essay items. Business teachers should review the readability of the tests before they are administered and review students' results after the tests have been administered. If students have clear understandings of the goals of the course and confidence that this is what they have learned, then tests and their results will be rewarding to everyone.

CONCLUSION

As people read through the numerous national reports concerning education published during the recent years, they come away with the feeling that "back to the basics" is the message. While it is hard to accept that message because it seems to decrease the time spent on learning business skills, no one can deny that everyone, including business students, must be able to read to survive. What this chapter has attempted to do is to give an overview of what reading is and how reading skills can be developed through business education by business teachers. Students come to business classes because they expect business teachers to prepare them to attain, maintain, and achieve upward mobility in employment; students can do this only if they can read— reading is their beginning.

CHAPTER 6

Understanding Applications of Organizational Communication Theory

HARRY FLAD

Data General Corporation, Westborough, Massachusetts

During the same period that corporate excellence became a theme in the business world, human resource systems as a tool for implementing business strategy became a popular topic. The two concepts are related through a focus on people resources as assets for doing business and through the proposition that people are directly related to a business organization's ability to compete effectively in the marketplace.

Increasingly, the emphasis in organizational training is being placed on employee involvement in order to increase productivity and to accelerate performance that can be measured against corporate goals and objectives. The highly competitive nature of the business environment requires that every advantage be developed in order to remain a healthy, profitable organization. The pressures that make human assets of critical importance include escalating international competition, increasing complexity and size of organizations, decreasing growth of markets, growing government involvement, increasing education of the work force, changing values of the work force, growing concern about career and life satisfaction, and changing demography in the work force.

Communication within organizations represents one of the primary forces that optimize the contributions of individual workers. This is accomplished by developing the skills of obtaining critical information, collaborating with others, and working in a team environment. These three represent opportunities through training to impact the effectiveness of an organization by developing skills and by empowering individuals to achieve the goals and objectives of an organization.

UNDERSTANDING TRAINING AND ORGANIZATIONAL COMMUNICATION

Although this chapter presents ideas from a training and development perspective in business, these same ideas can be used from a business education perspective in educational institutions. In addition to teaching the basic communication skills of listening, speaking, writing, and reading, business educators must accept responsibility for teaching organizational communication skills to their students. They can use approaches and techniques that are similar to, if not identical to, those that training and development specialists use to teach these skills.

Training and development within the human resource framework is seen as a tool for driving business strategies by recruiting, selecting, and developing people. It is done in order to accomplish the goals and objectives of an organization. A related issue to the development of people assets is the attention being given to training as a means to carry out individual development leading to improved performance on the job.

Another issue is transfer of learning. Transfer of learning to the job requires that the training experience is consistent with and supported by the objectives of top management, is encouraged by and approved by the manager of the person receiving the training, and has a positive impact on the expectations of peers about the effect that the training will have on the trainee. The issue of the transfer effect becomes critical in establishing the value of training in improving actual performance in a way that can be measured against corporate objectives and that can be observed in skill performances.

The work that has appeared about corporate excellence, the focus on people assets, and the research on different methods for reinforcing transfer support the perception that training can have an impact on business success; interestingly, evaluation of the impact of training is not widely practiced. However, evidence from research indicates that different methods of training are effective and that small effects of less than one half of one standard deviation have been shown to have substantial economic impact.[1]

This seems plausible when a person identifies the range of communication activities within an organizational environment that can be impacted by training programs. Such activities include, but probably would not be limited to, understanding perceptual differences among people, facilitating trust, handling interruptions, and managing conflict; managing individual communications, managing relationships on different organizational levels, improving communication among organizational groups, and developing networks among people within the organization; communicating visions, presenting personal ideas, developing presentations, and managing meetings; and providing communication performance feedback.

In order to impact communication issues, it is necessary to develop a strategy about training that goes beyond basic communication skills. Such a strategy within an organizational training environment requires a building-block approach, with course content linked both horizontally and vertically. Further, it should include a variety of areas that represent functional responsibilities in driving a business. Figure I shows one possible configuration for such a building-block approach.

A strategic approach to developing organizational skills around communication issues results in the ability to obtain critical information from others and the ability to develop the collaborative relationships necessary to function in a team environment. Such a strategy moves both horizontally and vertically

---

[1]Burke, Michael J., and Day, Russell R. "A Cumulative Study of the Effectiveness of Managerial Training." *Journal of Applied Psychology* 71:232-45; May 1986.

Courses

	Managing Conflict	Managing Change	Negotiation
Managerial Level	Managing Conflict	Managing Change	Negotiation
Professional Level	Managing Relationships	Developing Collaborative Relationships	Influencing Organizational Issues
Professional Skill-Building Level	Developing Communication Skills	Developing Writing Skills	Developing Presentation Skills

in an organization. Although vertical communication within an organization is often represented by extensive training programs focused on superior/subordinate relationships, this chapter has as its focus horizontal communication representing participative or team relationships. It is these relationships that are perceived as important and effective routes in influencing organizational issues.

OBTAINING CRITICAL INFORMATION

An organization consists of a myriad of networks between and among people who are involved in obtaining and sharing information. The extent to which a worker is able to develop relationships with fellow workers has a direct impact on his or her ability to perform and accomplish tasks. Key factors in developing individual relationships are a worker's communication style, how he or she reacts to tension, and how he or she develops communication strategies based on others' needs. A number of approaches have been created that address these three basic factors.

Many of these approaches have their roots in the managerial grid developed by Robert R. Blake and Jane S. Mouton.[2] Their work is a continuation of many decades of research on leadership that focuses on task accomplishment or concern for production and human relations or concern for people. Figure II shows that the grid brings these aspects together and identifies five types of resulting leadership.

The impoverished leadership type uses the minimum management effort required to get people to accomplish tasks. The country club leadership type emphasizes the needs of people in order to provide a comfortable work atmosphere. The middle of the road leadership type balances work and morale to obtain adequate work performance. The task leadership type emphasizes getting efficient work accomplished by arranging conditions of work so that people issues are minimized. The team leadership type gets work accomplished

---

[2]Blake, Robert R., and Mouton, Jane S. *The Managerial Grid*. Houston, Tex.: Gulf Publishing Co., 1964.

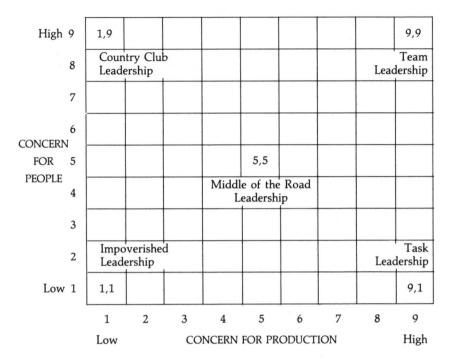

FIGURE II. Blake and Mouton's Managerial Grid

by committed people who have a common purpose and who demonstrate trust and respect.

Blake and Mouton focus on attitudes rather than behaviors, and the grid shows a predisposition toward styles rather than a measure of exhibited behaviors. The managerial grid has become a ubiquitous tool for identifying management styles, conflict management styles, and leadership styles. This approach also lends itself to identifying communication styles.

The four quadrants of the grid, when seen from a communication framework, contain important qualities for an organization as is evident from their characteristics. The quadrant where concern for both people and production is low (impoverished leadership type) is characterized by communication built around attention to detail, accuracy, and standards. The quadrant where concern for people is high and concern for production is low (country club leadership type) is characterized by communication focused around calm influence, strong social skills, and loyalty. The quadrant where concern for people is low and concern for production is high (task leadership type) is characterized by communication that makes fast decisions, gets things done, gets results, and is disciplined. The quadrant where concern for both people and production is high (team leadership type) is characterized by communication that is enthusiastic, creative, motivating, and goal oriented. The positive expressions of each of these styles permit people to interact effectively with fellow employees and to maintain the open communication networks necessary to accomplish work.

However, the relationship between tension and style can release negative reactions that restrict communication and reduce productivity. Figure III shows that tension has a curvilinear relationship to productivity that peaks at an optimal point and then declines.

FIGURE III. Relationship Between Productivity and Tension

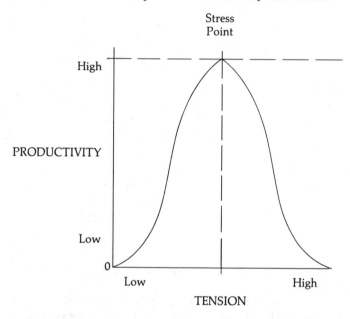

Beyond the stress point, additional tension can cause negative work behaviors if appropriate strategies are not used to manage the process of communication. The possibility of managing a person's own tension and meeting the needs of others allows for positive rather than negative interaction through three steps.

First, a person must understand his/her own disposition toward certain behaviors that are associated with his/her communication style. Second, a person must develop techniques for modifying expressions of his/her style and for identifying the styles of others. Third, a person must identify the needs of others in order to develop strategies for opening up communication with them so that information necessary to accomplish the work agenda can be obtained or shared.

Consequently, four backup or alternative styles emerge. In the quadrant where concern for both people and production are low (impoverished leadership style), the backup style of avoidance recognizes needs for exact details and standards. In the quadrant where concern for people is high and concern for production is low (country club leadership style), the backup style of acquiescence recognizes needs for security, credit for work, and group membership. In the quadrant where concern for people is low and concern for production is high (task leadership style), the backup style of autocracy recognizes needs for direct answers, power, and authority. In the quadrant where concern for both people and production is high (team leadership style), the backup style of attack behavior recognizes needs for social recognition and freedom.

By understanding various communication styles, recognizing how people react to tension, and developing communication strategies based on others' needs, people will be better able to obtain and share critical information.

COLLABORATING WITH OTHERS

The ability to collaborate with others evolves from possessing good interpersonal skills. Collaborating behavior is characterized by sharing information, synergistic problem solving, and goal-oriented team effort. Within the business context, the ability to work across organizational structures either in a matrix environment or as a member of a task-oriented team is the key ingredient for success in providing quality products in a timely fashion at a competitive cost.

The antithesis of the ability to collaborate is exhibited in dominating behaviors focusing around individual agendas or in avoidance behaviors resulting from feelings of impotence and lack of self-esteem. Dominating behaviors are characterized by autocratic behavior, attacking behavior, competing with other teams, and seeking personal advantage. Avoidance behaviors are characterized by seeking approval, avoiding confrontation, and holding back participation. Such antithetical behaviors more often than not are counterproductive to achieving the goals and objectives of an organization.

The rational skills used by task-oriented teams consist of problem-solving techniques or decision-making processes. The process skills or interpersonal skills are rooted in basic communication skills; namely, active listening and speaking, especially in the forms of clarifying, supporting, and confronting. One of the most exciting approaches to both understanding and developing the ability to collaborate in a team environment comes from the concept of group synergy. Synergistic approaches to decision making and problem solving have been known for the past two decades, and they utilize both rational and process skills to arrive at optimal strategies and solutions.

The concept of synergy is not easily understood by groups since the assumption, which has been demonstrated repeatedly, states that the group will arrive at better outcomes more often than the average individual. This becomes a more tenable idea when people participate in a synergistic exercise.

Although a person might be an expert on the issue facing the group, the other members of the group may have pieces of relevant information not known to the expert. Process skills allow for all of the sources of information that are necessary to develop a solution to be shared through collaborating behaviors. Further, process skills impact the rational process by bringing together all of the perspectives of the group. A person can simultaneously observe that dominating behaviors could restrict the information and that avoidance behaviors or acquiescence behaviors could result in the withholding of information.

The relationship between synergistic exercises and communication can be seen in the patterns among members of the group. Collaborating relationships from democratic communication are indicated by open communications among every member of the group. They allow for maximum interchange of information residing in the group. Dominating behaviors from autocratic communication are indicated by a one-way direction in communication patterns. Avoidance behaviors from avoidance communication are indicated by a lack of integration of all member inputs. Figure IV illustrates these three typical communication patterns.

FIGURE IV. Typical Communication Patterns

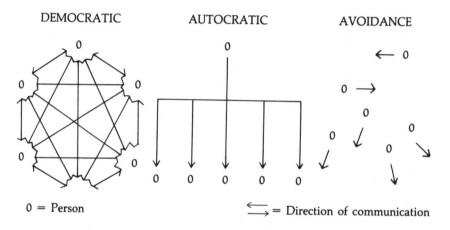

Demonstrating the process of synergy and the importance of open communication patterns can be accomplished by using synergistic exercises. The typical exercise consists of a rank order activity of 15 to 20 items done individually and as a group. The results of the individual and the group are then matched against a ranking of items based on expert opinion, which serves as a criterion. The lower the score, the greater the match to the expert's rankings since scores represent the adding of deviations. A perfect match would result in a zero score since there would be perfect matches in all rankings. Group scores typically are lower than the average of individual scores. Also, the existing synergy is indicated by the number of individual scores lower or better than the team score, with a zero score being the highest level of synergy. Figure V shows a completed version of a variation of a widely circulated synergistic exercise, and Figure VI shows the measurement of synergy if several groups complete the exercise at the same time.

Results from synergistic exercises are dramatic, and the experiential learning is highly effective. When the results are related back to individual styles, communication patterns, and process skills, the ability or inability to work in collaboration is demonstrated by all members of the group. The next step of relating communication behaviors to business issues and organizational teams becomes a relatively easy and worthwhile task.

FIGURE V. Completed Surviving on the Moon Exercise

Instructions: You are a member of a space crew that was originally scheduled to rendezvous with a mother ship on the lighted surface of the moon. Due to mechanical difficulties, your ship was forced to land about 200 miles from the rendezvous point. Many of the items on board were damaged during landing. Since survival depends on getting to the mother ship, you must select the most essential surviving items for your trip. Rank order the items in terms of their importance to allow your crew to rendezvous with the mother ship. Write the number 1 by the most important item and continue numbering items in terms of decreasing importance until all 15 items have been numbered.

SURVIVAL ITEMS	Step 1 Your Individual Ranking	Step 2 Your Crew's Ranking	Step 3 Survival Expert's Ranking*	Step 4 Difference Between Steps 1 and 3	Step 5 Difference Between Steps 2 and 3
Box of matches	15	14	15	0	1
Food concentrate	2	4	4	2	0
50 feet of nylon rope	7	7	6	1	1
Parachute silk	9	9	8	1	1
Portable heating unit	10	10	13	3	3
Two .45 calibre pistols	14	12	10	4	2
One case of powdered milk	6	5	11	5	6
Two 100 lb. tanks of oxygen	1	1	1	0	0
Map of the moon's constellation	3	6	3	0	3
Life raft	5	8	9	4	1
Magnetic compass	13	15	12	1	3
Five gallons of water	4	2	2	2	0
Signal flares	8	11	14	6	3
First aid kit containing injection needles	11	13	7	4	6
Solar-powered FM receiver-transmitter	12	3	5	7	2
			Totals (the lower the score the better)	40 Your Individual Score	32 Your Crew's Score

*The survival expert's rankings are provided after Steps 1 and 2 have been completed.

FIGURE VI. Measurement of Synergy on Surviving on the Moon Exercise

	Crew 1	Crew 2	Crew 3
Average Individual Score	49	37	42
Crew Score	32	31	28
Gain in Score	17	6	14
Number of Individual Scores			
Below Crew Score	0	1	0

Research supports the notion of optimal communication existing in a collaborating environment. Winning teams demonstrate collaborating behaviors with less evidence of competing or approval-seeking behaviors while losing teams show strong evidence of oppositional styles with competing and approval-seeking behaviors. It is of interest that all teams show similar individual scores. Further, the research shows that the characteristics of winning and losing teams are similar to executives' concepts of best manager and worst manager, reinforcing the view that strong organizational communications skills are valued and that power and avoidance are not highly regarded.[3]

Minimizing dominating and avoidance behaviors, using basic communication skills, and applying group synergy can result in optimal communication and, thus, collaboration with others.

WORKING IN A TEAM ENVIRONMENT

A number of programs exist that facilitate team building within organizations. Demonstrating the impact of communication processes on the effectiveness of group output can be accomplished through the use of human resource simulations. Simulations are defined as replications of real life situations and characteristically include roles, scenarios, and accounting systems.

Roles define players or decision makers and can be very specific or somewhat general depending on the objectives. Scenarios represent the task and include rules, task descriptions, and output descriptions. Accounting systems allow monitoring the progress of the simulation and include processes for providing feedback on the effects of decisions.

There are a multitude of simulations that vividly portray the effects of organizational communication within a business context. Among the more widely known are versions of the Lego exercise. The purpose of the exercise is to demonstrate how communication within the context of a team can be facilitated despite the formal and natural barriers of the organizational structure. Behaviors that can be observed among individual participants include complying, collaborating, obtaining and communicating information, competing between teams, and integrating of roles within a team environment.

---

[3]Lafferty, J. Clayton. *Level I: Life Styles.* Plymouth, Mich.: Human Synergistics, 1980.

The scenario for one of these versions involves building an exact replica of a model constructed from Legos, a brand of children's interlocking building blocks. The group is divided into two teams of at least nine players each. Each player is restricted by specific rules built around roles. Within a given time limit, a team may signal that it has completed the replica. At that point the replica is judged for accuracy. If the replica is an exact model, the team wins; if it is not, the other team wins by default.

The layout of the exercise provides artificial barriers simulating organization structures. Figure VII shows the placement of the players on each team. The roles represent various functions in creating the replica. The "lookers" may look at the model behind the screen and communicate to the "runners." The "runners" cannot see the model. They relay instructions from the "lookers" to the "builders." The "builders" receive instruction from the "lookers" and

FIGURE VII. Placement of Players for Lego Exercise

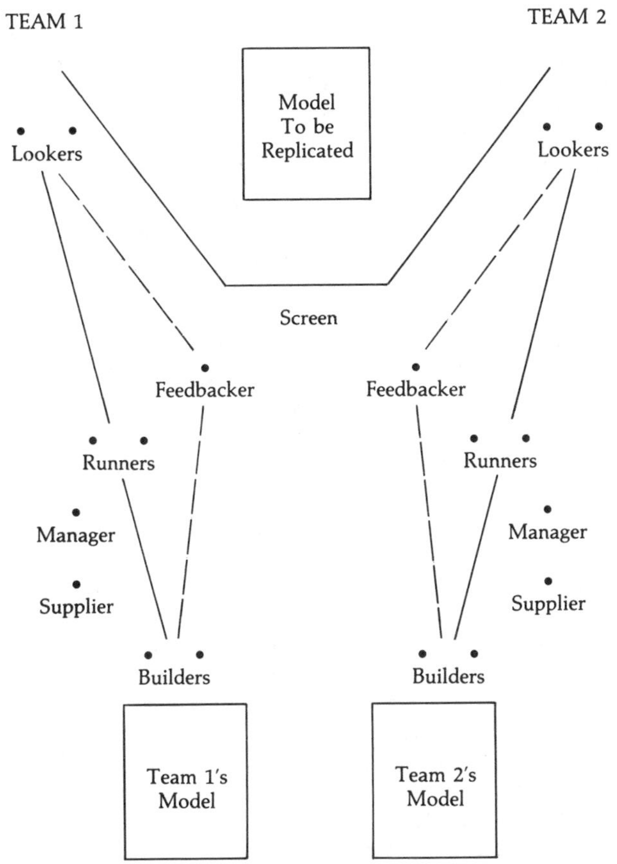

TEAM 1   TEAM 2

Lookers   Model   Lookers
                         To be
                         Replicated

                         Screen

          Feedbacker   Feedbacker

     Runners   Runners

 Manager   Manager

 Supplier   Supplier

     Builders   Builders

   Team 1's   Team 2's
   Model   Model

can obtain supplies from the "supplier." The "manager" can see the model and can call meetings, but he or she can only talk to the "feedbacker" between the meetings. The "supplier" can give six pieces at a time and can accept back unused pieces. He/she must also post the number of pieces obtained by the team during each five-minute interval. The "feedbacker" can see both models but can only answer questions with "that is right" or "that is not right." Anyone violating any rule must sit in a penalty box for 10 minutes.

Within the manager's role is the key to the exercise since only the manager can call a meeting. When all the team members attend the meeting, which is required, each player can transcend the role barriers. There are two issues about this power to call meetings that reside in the role of the manager. The first issue involves compliance. Usually a team will work for 15 or 20 minutes before its manager will call a meeting, and during that time the team will comply with the restrictions because of the fear of spending 10 minutes in the penalty box. The second issue involves communication. Team meetings provide a mechanism for periodically monitoring progress, resolving ambiguities about descriptions, and establishing linkages across all players, which is not allowed outside of meetings.

Characteristically, a winning team very quickly begins to call team meetings and to work in collaboration with its members in order to accomplish the task. In addition, managers of winning teams tend to use a participative approach. Managers of losing teams exhibit either excessive control or abdication behaviors, with the result that too few meetings are called to resolve issues. The resulting frustration of being in roles feels real, and it can be related to the workplace. The exercise provides an opportunity for emphasizing the value of team efforts in increasing the communication paths that are necessary to accomplish work tasks.

Although there are many ways to provide instruction about team building, simulations similar to the Lego exercise allow for experiential learning about issues encountered within a real business context. Participants are able to experience their typical behaviors in similar situations. In addition, opportunities are available while discussing the completed exercise to suggest ways of changing ineffective behaviors and empowering participants to become effective by developing workable communication strategies as team members.

CONCLUSION

Ensuring that all organization employees from the chief executive officer downward possess effective communication skills is no longer driven by humanistic considerations alone. The abilities to work with managers, peers, and subordinates to obtain critical information, to develop collaborating relationships, and to function as effective team players are often the determinants of career success. Without these skills, people offer little of value to an organization regardless of their technical or functional abilities. The development and application of organizational communication skills results in a concerned and committed work force that is successful and profitable in a highly competitive environment.

Part III

SPECIALIZATIONS: STRENGTHENING COMMUNICATION SKILLS

CHAPTER 7

Minimizing Communication Apprehension

EDWARD G. THOMAS and MARGARET HILTON BAHNIUK

Cleveland State University, Cleveland, Ohio

Most instructors can relate incidences in which their students exhibited such anxiety in class that they were ineffective communicators. The following examples could describe many of the students enrolled in business courses throughout the country.

> Judy prepares and rehearses her speech, but she is so frightened that she can't remember any part of it.

> Adam is a good student and knows the course material, but when a question is asked or when the class discusses the material, he does not contribute to the discussion.

> Kim has completed the research for a report, but she is so anxious that she is unable to write it.

These students are suffering from communication apprehension.

Communication apprehension, according to McCroskey, one of the pioneers in research on the subject, is "an individual's level of fear or anxiety associated with either real or anticipated communication with another person or persons."[1] One recent study of college students found that communication apprehension affects some 70 percent of the students at least occasionally, and over one-third of the students who experience it do so at least once weekly.[2] Communication apprehension often results in students who are nonparticipative, who are unpopular as social or work partners, and who receive low evaluations from teachers. Apprehensive students carry a double burden; not only must they learn the course material, but they must also confront the fear and anxiety associated with communicating with others, either face to face or in writing situations.

Is communication apprehension a personality trait or is it a learned fear? What does the research say about the phenomenon? What are the symptoms and effects of communication apprehension? What are some techniques that instructors can use to help students deal with their communication fears and anxieties? This chapter will answer these questions and suggest some strategies for helping students to minimize communication apprehension as they develop their communication skills.

---

[1]McCroskey, James C. "Oral Communication Apprehension: A Summary of Recent Theory and Research." *Human Communication Research* 4:78; Fall 1977.

[2]Bowers, John Waite. "Classroom Communication Apprehension: A Survey." *Communication Education* 35:373; October 1986.

REVIEW OF RESEARCH

Much of the research on communication apprehension has been aimed at defining and distinguishing between traitlike communication apprehension and situational communication apprehension. The former construct views communication apprehension as being a personality-like variable, giving a person a relatively constant orientation toward a given form of communication.[3] Note that the term *traitlike* is used here; a true trait of an individual is not subject to change. On the other hand, a traitlike characteristic, such as oral communication apprehension, is subject to change.

Situational communication apprehension is statelike, representing "the reactions of an individual to communicating with a given individual or group of individuals at a given time."[4] Thus, the level of situational communication apprehension varies from context to context or situation to situation.

McCroskey has described these two types of communication apprehension as lying on a continuum with traitlike communication apprehension at one end and situational communication apprehension at the other end.[5] Obviously, between the two would be a number of communication-apprehension models incorporating varying degrees of traitlike and situational communication-apprehension characteristics. The research indicates that most humans exhibit some traitlike communication-apprehension behaviors and some situational communication-apprehension behaviors. The majority of people are able to adjust to or overcome their communication-apprehension problems. Only in a minority of cases is communication apprehension so severe as to be termed abnormal.

There have been two schools of thought about what causes traitlike communication apprehension: heredity and environment. That is, some people believe a person is born with communication apprehension; others believe that a person learns it. Most early writers proposed that communication apprehension was a learned trait; in recent years, research has tended to show that the situation is not that simple. Research with newborn infants and identical and fraternal twins has shown that some traits, such as sociability, are present shortly after birth and are much more alike in identical twins than in fraternal twins.[6] Thus, the research supports the contention that heredity may be a contributing cause of traitlike communication apprehension.

Research into the environmental causes of traitlike communication apprehension has been relatively unsatisfactory. Since there are massive problems associated with conducting experimental research on traitlike communication apprehension, most of the studies in this area depend on correlational approaches. Because correlational techniques typically are not used for inferring causality, much of the writing about traitlike communication

---

[3]McCroskey, James C. "Oral Communication Apprehension: A Reconceptualization." *Communication Yearbook 6.* (Edited by M. Burgoon.) Beverly Hills, Calif.: Sage, 1982. p. 147.

[4]*Ibid.*, p. 149.

[5]*Ibid.*, p. 147.

[6]McCroskey, James C., and Richmond, J. P. *The Quiet Ones: Communication Apprehension and Shyness.* Dubuque, Iowa: Gorsuch Scarisbrick, 1980. p. 6.

apprehension is in the realm of speculation.[7] Much more satisfactory results have been obtained from research on the causes of situational communication apprehension. Buss, for example, has identified the following elements in a situation that can result in higher levels of communication apprehension:

1. Novelty—the individual is unsure how to behave in the unfamiliar situation.

2. Formality—the more formal the situation, the more narrow the range of acceptable behavior.

3. Subordinate status—in most situations, appropriate behavior is defined by the person having the higher status.

4. Conspicuousness—situations in which a person feels conspicuous (e.g., giving a speech, being a new person in a group, etc.) tend to increase communication apprehension.

5. Unfamiliarity—in general, people are more comfortable when communicating with people they know; communication apprehension tends to increase when the degree of familiarity decreases.

6. Dissimilarity—in general, people are more comfortable when communicating with people who are similar to themselves; however, there are exceptions. Some people are uncomfortable communicating with peers in situations where the peers will be evaluating them.

7. Degree of attention—most people are comfortable with a moderate degree of attention from others. Communication apprehension increases when people are either stared at or completely ignored.[8]

Daly and Hailey have described two additional causes of situational communication apprehension: degree of evaluation and prior history.[9] According to the researchers, people experience more communication apprehension when being evaluated than when no evaluation is apparent. However, not everyone reacts to evaluation in the same way. Research on writing communication apprehension shows that good writers tend to improve when being evaluated, but poor writers tend to do worse.[10]

Daly and Hailey also propose that prior history is an important element in situational communication apprehension. A person who has experienced failure in the past is likely to be apprehensive about failing in the future.

A considerable portion of the body of research on communication apprehension has been devoted to the development and validation of methods for measuring communication apprehension. Historically, researchers have used three methods to determine the existence of communication apprehension: observer ratings, devices for measuring physiological changes, and self-report scales. Researchers in the area of observer ratings say that communication apprehension can result in observable human behavior; however, critics say high levels of communication apprehension are likely to result in withdrawal or avoidance behavior, neither of which leads to easily observed communi-

---

[7]McCroskey, "Oral Communication Apprehension: A Reconceptualization," p. 153.

[8]Buss, A. H. *Self-Consciousness and Social Anxiety*. San Francisco: W. H. Freeman, 1980.

[9]Daly, J. A., and Hailey, J. L. *Putting the Situation into Writing Research: Situational Parameters of Writing Apprehension as Disposition and State*. Paper presented at the National Council of Teachers of English Convention, Cincinnati, 1980.

[10]*Ibid.*

cation behavior. In addition, gathering data through observer ratings is labor intensive, time-consuming, and therefore, relatively expensive.

Measuring physiological changes during communication activities is also expensive, depending as it does on the use of fairly sophisticated mechanical and electronic instruments to measure such things as elevated heart rate, increased muscle tension, skin temperature, and brain wave activity. It is also difficult to use such devices in all types of communication contexts.

Because the first two methods provide only indirect evidence of communication apprehension and the measures are not often significantly correlated, much of the research has focused on self-report scales. McCroskey developed the most noteworthy self-report instrument—the Personal Report of Communication Apprehension (PRCA)—for measuring oral communication apprehension. There are several versions of this instrument available. All the versions use 5-step, Likert-type response formats. Samples of these instruments can be found in a 1970 issue of *Speech Monographs.*[11]

The most recently developed 24-item version includes 6 items for each of four contexts: speaking in public, talking in meetings or classes, talking in small groups, and talking in dyads (i.e., two-person groups). Participants are asked to indicate the degree to which the statements apply to them by marking whether they "Strongly Agree," "Agree," "Are Undecided," "Disagree," or "Strongly Disagree" with the various statements. The instrument includes such statements as:

I have no fear of facing an audience.

While participating in a conversation with a new acquaintance, I feel very nervous.

I look forward to expressing my opinion in meetings.[12]

Most of the research on communication apprehension, such as McCroskey's, has focused on oral communication apprehension. However, some work has been done in the area of measuring writing apprehension. Daly and Miller's Writing Apprehension Test was developed in 1975 to measure writing anxiety. The 26-item instrument is patterned after the McCroskey instrument (the PRCA) and asks participants to rate the degree to which they agree with such statements as:

I avoid writing.

I have no fear of my writing being evaluated.

I look forward to writing down my ideas.[13]

A shorter 20-item version of the instrument has been created for use outside the writing class.

The Writing Apprehension Test has been found to have only a moderate correlation with McCroskey's measures. Research has shown that apprehension

[11]McCroskey, James C. "Measures of Communication-Bound Anxiety." *Speech Monographs* 37:269-77; 1970.

[12]McCroskey, James C. *An Introduction to Rhetorical Communication.* Fourth edition. Englewood Cliffs, N.J.: Prentice-Hall, 1982.

[13]Daly, John A., and Miller, Michael D. "The Empirical Development of an Instrument To Measure Writing Apprehension." *Research in the Teaching of English* 9:242-49; 1975.

about one form of communication is a poor predictor of apprehension about any other form. No instrument yet exists to measure all forms of communication.

SYMPTOMS AND EFFECTS OF COMMUNICATION APPREHENSION

McCroskey describes three behavioral response patterns when high levels of communication apprehension are present: communication avoidance, communication withdrawal, and communication disruption.[14] The most common behavioral response to communication apprehension is avoidance. When confronted with an undesirable situation, people typically must choose between overcoming the situation (fighting it) or avoiding the situation (fleeing from it). For those with high communication apprehension, "flight" is the most typical pattern of response.

Because avoidance is not always possible, separate behavioral responses have evolved for those instances when the high communication-apprehension individual cannot flee. Under these circumstances, the most typical response is withdrawal, either completely (engaging in absolute silence) or partially (giving the shortest possible response).

The third type of response is communication disruption, when the high communication-apprehension individual's communication performance is poor. It should be noted here that low levels of communication performance could also be caused by low levels of communication skill. Thus, one must be careful not to infer too much from poor communication performance.

From the viewpoint of the individual who experiences communication apprehension, there are both internal and external manifestations. Inside, the person typically experiences discomfort, feelings of anxiety, and other signs of stress, such as "butterflies in the stomach." In the oral communication situation, some external symptoms are excessive perspiring, shaking hands and legs, a tight or nervous voice, and constantly shifting feet.

Individuals with writing apprehension seem to share a number of characteristics. They consistently fail to turn in written work. They do not attend class when writing is required. They seldom voluntarily enroll in courses in which writing is known to be demanded. They have a fear of evaluation of their written communication. The last characteristic is the most descriptive of apprehensive writers since the other three symptoms could be the result of other factors. For example, chronic procrastinators may fail to turn in work; lazy students may avoid courses requiring much writing.

Internally, the apprehensive writer may experience feelings of foreboding and other forms of stress. In extreme cases "writers block" may occur. This condition, when the writer's mind essentially becomes a blank, causes the writer to be unable to think of anything to write. Many writers occasionally experience short periods of time when nothing "comes to them." However, writers with communication apprehension experience this situation often.

---

[14]McCroskey, "Oral Communication Apprehension: A Reconceptualization," p. 164.

STRATEGIES FOR MINIMIZING
COMMUNICATION APPREHENSION

Foss has described methods that have traditionally been used in working with communication-apprehensive students.[15] Based on the assumption that extreme anxiety about communication is largely learned, several behavior modification approaches have been used successfully. The most frequently used approach is systematic desensitization, which operates on the principle that pairing anxiety-producing events with pleasurable or positive occurrences causes the fear-filled aspects of the former to be diminished. "The technique involves identifying and ranking the events that produce anxiety, teaching a method of muscle relaxation, then pairing the feared events with the incompatible deep relaxation."[16] This method works because it is impossible for a person to be tense and relaxed at the same time.

Biofeedback and hypnosis are other techniques that are sometimes used in conjunction with systematic desensitization. The biofeedback method teaches students to control certain physiological processes, such as heart rate and body tension. Hypnosis involves placing a person in a trance during which time certain suggestions can be made about altering posthypnotic behavior.

Systematic desensitization, biofeedback, hypnosis, and similar techniques require highly trained people to guide their use. Most teachers do not have the training necessary for using these techniques. They may wish, however, to refer students with especially serious cases of communication apprehension to professionals who do use these types of methods.

Two approaches to helping students with high levels of communication apprehension that most classroom teachers can use are cognitive restructuring and skills training. Cognitive restructuring involves helping students change the way they think about or relate to the act of communicating.

> When this technique is applied to communication anxiety, students are asked to alter their apprehension cognitively by identifying negative self-statements that they make about their communication and by substituting more positive, anxiety-reducing coping statements for them. For example, the student who typically says, "I'm going to sound stupid" when anticipating an upcoming speaking assignment can learn to say instead, "I've done my homework on this topic."[17]

Skills training is based on the assumption that a major source of anxiety comes from not knowing how to deal with a particular communication situation. A part of the skills training approach relies on instructors presenting the relevant course content and giving students opportunities to practice and develop their communication skills in a variety of situations. Another part of skills training is helping students decide on communication goals to be achieved within the course. The emphasis is always on developing skills, not on treating anxiety.

---

[15]Foss, Karen A. "Overcoming Communication Anxiety." *Improving Speaking and Listening Skills.* (Edited by Rebecca B. Rubin.) San Francisco: Jossey-Bass, 1983.

[16]*Ibid.,* p. 26.

[17]*Ibid.,* p. 29.

Teachers work most often with students who could be characterized as having low to moderate levels of communication apprehension. Students with very severe problems are usually referred to professionals. Part of the reason for this is that the techniques which work best with persons having low to moderate communication apprehension do not work well with those who suffer from the highest levels of anxiety.

There are a number of things a classroom teacher can do to help communication-apprehensive students. The following suggestions incorporate some aspects of cognitive restructuring and skills training:

1. Determine the levels of communication apprehension in the classroom.

2. Help students recognize their fears as normal.

3. Create a supportive environment.

4. Provide good models.

5. Help students learn to relax.

6. Give students technical advice.

The remainder of the chapter is devoted to offering specific practical suggestions in each of these areas.

Determine the levels of communication apprehension. It is important to know the degree to which your students experience communication apprehension. Because observations of behavior are not reliable indicators, the best way to determine this is to let the students tell you. Administer and score a version of McCroskey's Personal Report of Communications Apprehension (PRCA) or his Personal Report of Public Speaking Apprehension (PRPSA).[18] For writing students, administer Daly and Miller's Writing Apprehension Test (WAT).[19] Based on the results of the assessment(s), determine to what extent you need to make a special effort to help alleviate communication apprehension.

Help students recognize their fears as normal. Share with students information about how widespread the fear of public speaking is. Virtually everyone who has had to make an oral presentation to a group has experienced some degree of stage fright. The fear of public speaking is so widespread that the respondents in one research study ranked "speaking before a group" as a greater fear than the "fear of death." The survey, which included over 2,500 male and female adults, revealed that the following were the 10 most highly rated fears:

Item	Percent of Respondents
1. Speaking before a group	40.6%
2. Height	32.0
3. Insects	22.1
4. Financial problems	22.0
5. Deep water	21.5

[18]McCroskey, "Measures of Communication-Bound Anxiety," pp. 272-76.

[19]Daly and Miller, *op. cit.*, pp. 242-49.

6. Sickness	18.8
7. Death	18.7
8. Flying	18.3
9. Loneliness	13.6
10. Dogs	11.2[20]

A more recent study asked respondents to indicate the social situations that they most feared. The responses were as follows:

Greatest Fear	Percent Naming
A party with strangers	74%
Giving a speech	70
Asked personal questions in public	65
Meeting a date's parents	59
First day on a new job	59
Victim of a practical joke	56
Talking with someone in authority	53
Job interview	46
Formal dinner party	44
Blind date	42[21]

Tell students about times when you were nervous before giving a speech or making a class presentation. Read to them the item from the July 30, 1981, issue of *The New York Times*, (page 1, column 3) that describes how the nervous Lady Diane Spencer mixed up the four given names of her about-to-be-husband, Prince Charles. Find newspaper and magazine articles—and there are many—in which famous actors and actresses admit their feelings of nervousness before every performance. Show a videotape of any televised awards program (e.g., the Academy Awards, the Emmys, or the Grammys) and note how nervous and flustered both the presenters and the recipients are. Encourage students to openly and honestly admit their feelings of apprehension about oral communication situations.

If your students are apprehensive about writing, you should help them understand that almost everyone experiences some degree of apprehension about writing at one time or another. Professional writers often comment that the scariest thing they ever face is a blank page in the typewriter (perhaps now it is a blank screen on the word processor). Discuss the phenomenon of "writer's block" with the students. Show them books and articles that illustrate methods by which others have overcome writing problems. Continually let students know that writing apprehension is not unusual.

Create a supportive environment. Because the environment in which communication occurs is so important, the teacher should create and sustain

---

[20]"What Are Americans Afraid Of?" *The Bruskin Report.* New Brunswick, N.J.: R. H. Bruskin Associates, July 1973. p. 1.

[21]Lucas, Stephen E. *The Art of Public Speaking.* Second edition. New York: Random House, 1986. p. 11.

a supportive classroom environment from the first day of the class. Students need to get to know each other and become relatively comfortable in the classroom setting.

Research with oral-communication-apprehensive students has shown that small-group activities can help to "break the ice." At first, use small-group activities to allow group members to get acquainted. Then, introduce activities where group members begin to make short presentations about themselves or their interests to only the group. Gradually move to a situation where each group is responsible for making a presentation to the rest of the class.

To eliminate some of the pressure, avoid evaluating these early efforts. Just encourage a lot of communication. Give positive verbal support to those who participate well. Give some gentle encouragement to those who hold back. If grading is necessary, consider using only "satisfactory" and "unsatisfactory" at first.

When the oral communication assignment involves individuals making presentations, the teacher should seek an appropriate balance between offering suggestions for improvement and giving praise for a job well done. Whenever possible, the positive aspects of a presentation should be emphasized. Serious shortcomings should be discussed in a private conversation with the student. Too much negative oral feedback during the class may cause avoidance behavior.

Building a supportive environment is also important where written communication is the focus. The teacher may start the students off with some short in-class writing assignments. Note the ones who appear to be having problems. Offer them some suggestions of things to write or ways to write them. Make sure that your instructions to the students are clearly stated. Encourage them to ask questions to clarify the assignment.

Throughout the course, focus on developing a positive classroom climate by emphasizing success rather than failure, by setting up expectations of success, and by giving positive reinforcement. Unfortunately, the easiest way to evaluate assignments is to concentrate on the negatives, the errors, and the suggestions for improvement. Positive comments should also be a part of class discussions and oral conferences with students. Apprehensive writing students need to experience positive reinforcement and success with their writing.

Another way to build a supportive climate for writing-apprehensive students is to provide opportunities for writing when the exercises will not be evaluated. Most writing-apprehensive students are afraid of how others will respond to their writing, so they need many opportunities to develop writing in a nonevaluative setting. Students need to be told ahead of time that the writing will not be evaluated, so they will feel freer about their writing. If grading is necessary, consider using a "satisfactory/unsatisfactory" assessment scheme for the early writing assignments.

In addition to delaying evaluation, give graduated assignments so students can experience success on one task before going on to a more difficult assignment. Start with short, easy-to-do assignments. Gradually increase the length and complexity.

The teacher should also consider the use of structured and unstructured assignments. Research has shown that communication-apprehensive students succeed better when the assignment is highly structured, giving them a lot of guidance in how to complete the task. However, high structure may be inhibiting to nonapprehensive students. One solution is to provide alternative assignments, some with a lot of built-in structure and some with less structure. Then, students may select the assignment that gives them the desired amount of freedom.

Provide good models. There is some evidence that oral communication apprehension is developed, in part, by people watching others who are nervous presenters. "From watching others, presenters acquire the belief that nervousness is appropriate even if undesirable."[22] To help students "unlearn" such behavior, provide them with positive role models. Let them watch live, filmed, or videotaped models who are good speakers. Point out what the best techniques are. Discuss the lack of obvious nervous behavior. If the facilities are available, videotape students as they make presentations. Edit the videotapes so that only the best portions are available for playback. Discuss how the behaviors exhibited could be incorporated in future presentations.

Modeling is also possible in the writing class. Provide students with samples of good writing. Discuss the features that distinguish the well-written assignment from the poorly written one. Where possible, use samples of good writing from the class members themselves. Share with students your own written responses to various assignments. Write out several versions of a particular assignment to illustrate the fact that there are usually many acceptable approaches to a writing problem. Keep the emphasis on providing positive models of behavior that students can imitate.

Help students learn to relax. Many of the symptoms of communication apprehension would likely disappear if students would just learn to relax. The instructor can help in this regard by teaching some relaxation techniques. It is not possible to go into the specifics of relaxation training here, but there are many excellent books and articles available on the subject. Read some of these and choose one or two techniques to use with students. The following is a description of one technique that is widely used:

> Sit in a comfortable chair away from any distractions and bright lights. Start by taking several deep breaths and exhaling slowly. With each breath, deepen the relaxation. To go through the progressive relaxation process, start by focusing your attention on the muscles in your feet. Flex the muscles and then let them relax. Do the same thing with your legs, then gradually move up through your body, flexing the muscles and relaxing them. When you are thoroughly relaxed, take a few minutes to enjoy the experience; then begin thinking about the speech.[23]

While in this state of relaxation, the student is typically advised to visualize himself/herself standing in front of the audience, delivering the speech in

---

[22]Page, William T. "Helping the Nervous Presenter: Research and Prescriptions." *Journal of Business Communication* 22:12; Spring 1985.

[23]Hasling, John. *The Message, the Speaker, the Audience.* Third edition. New York: McGraw-Hill Book Co., 1982. p. 82.

the desired fashion. The important thing is for the student to associate the positive image with the feeling of relaxation. This association will carry over to the actual delivery of the speech, giving the student a more relaxed feeling.

Relaxation techniques are also valuable for writing-apprehensive students. Obviously, it is the picture of the desired performance or result that will be different.

Give students technical advice. Most teachers give technical advice to students. That is the major focus of much teaching about communicating. The following is a compilation of advice gathered from many sources. Pass this sort of information along to students. Supplement the list with other items or examples from your reading or experience.

Oral Communication Tips

1. Prepare thoroughly. There is no substitute for being well prepared. Advance planning covers not only the speech but your manner of dress as well. Decide ahead of time what you will wear.

2. Practice the speech. Ask one or more friends or family members to give honest feedback.

3. Prepare well-organized notes. Number the pages or cards so that they can be put back in order quickly if they are dropped.

4. Visualize what you want to do. Get a mental picture of how you will look as you confidently present the speech. Get this mental picture every time you think of your speech.

5. Focus on communicating with the audience. Concentrate entirely on getting the message across to the audience.

6. Learn a relaxation technique for use before and/or during a talk.

7. Prepare a good introduction. Getting off to a good start usually helps dissipate the feelings of nervousness.

8. Use visual aids. They are attention getting, they can serve as your set of notes, and they can be used to direct attention away from you to the points on the poster or screen.

9. Get a good night's sleep. A last-minute push will probably make you more nervous.

10. Get to the speaking site ahead of time. This will help you avoid any last-minute surprises. Decide ahead of time what you will do if there is an equipment problem or the room is not set up as you expected.

11. Avoid eating a heavy meal just prior to the presentation.

12. Do not schedule other important activities on the day of the presentation.

13. Remember that the members of the audience want you to do well. They want to acquire the information or ideas you have to offer.

14. Remember that perfection is rarely achieved. Be satisfied with making your best effort.

Written Communication Tips

1. Control your writing environment. This would include choosing the correct instrument (pen, pencil, typewriter, word processor), choosing the right place

to be most productive (the kitchen, a study, the library), and choosing the right time of the day to write (depending on whether you are a "day" or "night" person).

2. Divide the work into stages. Many students have difficulty tackling a writing problem because they see how much work is needed to finish the entire project. Break the project up into segments and tackle only one part at a time (writing the introduction or making an outline, for example).

3. Write fast for the first draft; just try to get your major ideas on paper. Don't be concerned about proper word choice, grammar, or punctuation at first. These items should be corrected in the revising stage. Also, don't put in the footnotes or other supplementary parts of the paper during the first draft.

4. Be sure to have your purpose clearly in mind. When you get stuck, go back to the purpose and reread it. This will usually get you back on track.

5. Complete most, if not all, of your research before you begin writing. Then, after you have quickly written the first draft, do more research, if it is needed, to fill in the gaps.

6. Outline the topic before you begin so you know the order of presentation.

7. Start writing the easiest section first. If the conclusion is easier to write than the introduction, write it first and write the introduction last.

8. Reward yourself with special treats (a telephone call, a snack, a walk) after major sections have been written. This gives you an incentive to continue.

9. Set deadlines (decide to write a certain number of pages before you stop or decide to write nonstop for a particular period of time).

10. Work ahead of schedule so you allow plenty of time for the revising and proofreading stages. This helps lower the stress level.

11. Schedule writing time as a part of your daily routine; otherwise, your inclination may be to put it off until later.

12. If you are having difficulty starting, record your thoughts first on a tape recorder.

13. If you are having difficulty starting a new section, reread the last section; this will often help the thoughts start to flow again. Read a difficult section aloud to hear how it sounds.

14. If you get stuck and can't seem to write another word, change writing instruments or change locations. This will sometimes give you a fresh slant.

15. Know when to let go of the writing. Many famous authors relate how they avoid reading their books after they have been published because they always find parts they want to revise. You can always find things to change. There comes a time when you must say, "This may not be perfect, but it is good. I've spent enough time on it."

CONCLUSION

Since communication apprehension is highly associated with ineffective communication, it must be a central concern of instructors. Developing an awareness of the causes of communication apprehension and being willing to communicate caring and concern to students who suffer from it seem to be the critical first steps in treating the problem.

CHAPTER 8

Building Communication Skills with Technologies

CAROL A. LUNDGREN
Utah State University, Logan

Business communication has become, to a large extent, electronic communication. Microcomputers are used in several ways to facilitate written business communications—to prepare written correspondence and reports, to create visual aids, and to send electronic messages. Telecommunications software and electronic bulletin boards allow users to access vast databases for information on research topics or for use in daily decision making. Other electronic media such as dictation equipment, teleconference networks, videotape/disk technology, and electronic telephone equipment facilitate oral communications. Thus, both writing and speaking have entered a new era, one in which students need special skills to use the technology effectively for business communication.

The technology used in business communication also requires teachers to focus more of their instruction on the process used to create written and oral messages. In other words, since technology has become an integral part of communication, the technology used to create the message is as important as the message itself. Business communication teachers today need to know what technology students will be using in the business world and how they will use it. Further, teachers should help students develop the skills they need to use that technology proficiently.

BUILDING WRITING SKILLS WITH MICROCOMPUTER TECHNOLOGY

Contrary to what many students would like to believe, a personal computer has no magical properties. It cannot turn a poor writer into a good one, but it can make the writing task easier and more efficient. Word processing programs make accurate typing and editing easier. Proofreading and spelling software help writers check the accuracy of their work. Punctuation and grammar programs draw attention to writing weaknesses and inconsistencies. Telecommunications software reduces the time required to gather information. Computer graphics packages help writers create attractive and informative illustrations for reports and oral presentations.

Pearce pointed out several differences between preparing business communications on a computer and by the pencil and paper method.[1] First,

---

[1]Pearce, C. Glenn. "Business Writing: Computer Instruction vs. Traditional Methods." *Business Education Forum* 40:11-12; May 1986.

students must be concerned not only with the content of the message but also with the operation of the software they are using. Second, students can either edit as they write or complete an entire document and then edit it— either approach is equally efficient on a computer. Third, editing a computer document is easier than editing a handwritten one, assuming that the student is a proficient operator. Fourth, spelling and proofreading software can improve the accuracy of written documents, again, if the student is proficient in using them. Fifth, computers can be much more frustrating instruments than pens and pencils. Consequently, the student who lacks confidence may become even more apprehensive about his/her writing ability when a computer is used. These differences provide an excellent basis for examining how teachers can use the computer to improve writing skills.

Using word processing software for business communications. Since letters, memos, and reports are common forms of business communications prepared on computers, word processing software has become a tool for the writing process. Word processing programs allow the user to type with less concern about typing errors and to skip around the text to revise and format the document. Words can be deleted, added, or moved at the whim of the writer; lines can be centered automatically; page numbers can be printed in the appropriate place on each page automatically; and lines can be right justified if the writer desires. These features are strong motivators for using the computer to prepare written documents, and no one disputes the wisdom of using word processing *if one knows how.* The problem that arises in the business communication course is that many students do not know how to use the software well enough to produce quality documents.

Business communication teachers handle the differences in the word processing proficiency of their students in several ways. In some cases teachers give their students a crash course in word processing before they begin their writing assignments. In other cases, students who take business communication must have a certain level of word processing, or at least typing, skill before they enroll in the course. In still other cases, teachers leave the decision to use the computer to their students. Regardless of the approach teachers use, word processing skill becomes an evaluation factor.

Probably no teacher today would consider penmanship in determining the grade a student receives on a report. However, format errors and spacing inconsistencies in computer-produced documents cannot be ignored because those errors affect the quality of the document. Students develop substantial skill in using a pen—at least in a technical sense—before they begin to compose. They seldom have the same skill level or knowledge of the technology before they begin using microcomputers for writing. Even if students use word processing software proficiently and make revisions accurately, that does not guarantee that their documents will be better written; it guarantees only that their documents will be more attractive. In any case, the evaluation process must include the appearance of the written document. Therefore, if students are allowed to use word processing software for business communications, they need to know how to use it. Otherwise, they should be required to prepare their assignments on the typewriter or in handwriting.

Teachers can help students develop word processing skills by explaining how to use the software to format documents and check the accuracy of the message.

Simplifying the formatting process. Two new approaches to heading format and spacing in reports are gaining acceptance in word processing circles. These approaches are more efficient and easier for students to use than the traditional methods.

The traditional approach to heading format includes several levels that begin with a centered heading with all letters capitalized and proceed through centered, side, and paragraph headings that are underlined with only certain words capitalized. The new approach is to capitalize all letters in any level heading and let placement determine the importance of the heading. In other words, a first-level heading would be all caps and centered; a second-level heading would be all caps and flush left; and a third-level heading would be all caps at the beginning of a paragraph and followed by a period. In spacing reports, usually the body of the report is double-spaced. Traditionally, triple-spacing is used before and after centered headings and before side headings. The new approach is to quad-space (two double-spaces) before and after a centered heading and double-space before a side heading; in this way only a setting for double-spacing is needed for the entire report. These two approaches make formatting on the microcomputer easier for novices because many of the control characters required by some word processing programs are eliminated.

Students should be given a sheet of standard format instructions for setting margins, numbering pages, placing headings, spacing, and documenting. The latter presents some special problems. Since reports with bottom-of-the-page footnotes are difficult for even experienced word processing operators to prepare, students should be taught to use American Psychological Association author-date references, especially if they have minimal word processing skill.

Formatting improves the appearance of written documents. However, a more important part of the writing process is recognizing errors in style, tone, wording, grammar, spelling, and punctuation. Several word processing programs are available that help writers find these errors and offer suggestions for making revisions.

Using composition analysis programs. Writer's Workbench is one example of a computer program that analyzes several aspects of composition. Although Writer's Workbench has been used in English departments for some time, it has not gained widespread acceptance in business communication courses. The program provides a great deal of information if all the subprograms are used, but the writer needs to know how to interpret the information. For example, the FINDBE subprogram highlights forms of the verb *be* anywhere that they appear. This information is useful if students understand that those verb forms should be replaced with action verbs in some cases and can recognize the proper use of auxiliary verbs. The following list describes some of the subprograms that could be useful for writing instruction, explains what students need to know to use them effectively, and suggests what supplementary instruction teachers should provide.

DICTION highlights wordy phrases and words that exceed a certain number of characters. Students should understand what constitutes a wordy phrase and why such phrases increase miscommunication. Also, because long words are not necessarily poor word choices, vocabulary instruction should supplement the use of this program. SUGGEST works with DICTION by printing possible revisions for the wordy phrases and long words. If DICTION is used, then SUGGEST should also be used along with some discussion about the revisions.

CHECK highlights commonly confused words such as *affect* and *effect*. A vocabulary review should accompany the use of this program to help students improve word choice.

ABSTRACT highlights abstract words, such as *personality*, and prints the percentage of abstract words in the document. Students need to know the difference between abstract words and concrete words and when to use them.

GRAMMAR highlights split infinitives. Students need to know what a split infinitive is, why it should be avoided, and how to change it.

PUNCTUATION highlights a lowercase letter if it appears at the beginning of a sentence and highlights quotation marks and parentheses if they do not appear in sets of two. This program is a useful editing tool but does little to improve punctuation. Students still need a review of grammar and punctuation rules.

SPELLING highlights words that are not in the Writer's Workbench dictionary. Students need to know that the highlighted words are ones that the program does not recognize and that those words are not necessarily misspelled. They also need to know that misuse of homophones such as *hear* and *here* or omitted words will not be found. Therefore, proofreading instruction should supplement the use of this program.

STYLE prints the average sentence length (in number of words), average word length (in number of characters), and the number of words in the shortest and longest sentences. PROSE assesses readability and prints the grade level required to read the document; indicates the number of simple, compound, and complex sentences; and highlights sentences in passive voice. Both of these programs require knowledge of how readability formulas are derived and knowledge of sentence elements.

Writer's Workbench is only one of many programs that attempt to check grammar and punctuation. Programs that will appear in the future, according to business literature, may actually be able to analyze the grammatical correctness of a sentence.[2]

A program that analyzes composition could be very useful in reducing the tedium of checking student papers for certain stylistic errors, but it cannot totally replace teacher feedback. Research has shown that this type of program does no more to improve student writing than traditional teaching of editing skills.[3] Also, the time required to teach students to use the software cuts into

---

[2]Munter, Mary. "Using the Computer in Business Communications Courses." *Journal of Business Communication* 23:31-41; Winter 1986.

[3]Ober, Scot, and Kocar, Marcella J. "The Effect of Student Use of a Computerized Writing Analysis Program on Writing Achievement." *Delta Pi Epsilon Journal* 28:99-106; Spring 1986.

valuable class time. Teachers need to weigh the benefits they hope their students will gain by using the program against this serious disadvantage. Probably the main attraction of composition analysis programs is their potential for reducing the time required to mark papers. Experts have found spelling and proofreading programs more beneficial for both students and teachers.[4] These programs usually require less instruction in their use and do improve the overall quality of student papers.

Using spelling and proofreading programs. Most word processing programs have accompanying spelling or proofreading programs. These programs are easy to learn and efficient to use. The disadvantage in using them, of course, is that they cannot make judgments. Each spelling program has a dictionary, often of many thousands of words. As the program goes through a document, it checks each word against its dictionary. If a word is not found, the word is highlighted, and the user is asked to accept the word, change it, or add it to the dictionary.

The greatest advantage of spelling programs is that they can find typographical errors; the greatest disadvantage is that their use may encourage students to neglect their own proofreading. Since spelling programs will not find transposed words or words that sound alike but are spelled differently, they are not a good substitute for careful proofreading. Students should be taught to proofread their written documents for meaning, so that a sentence which reads "The committee herd the report from the patience" doesn't escape detection and correction.

Helping apprehensive writers. The computer can become a formidable obstacle to students who lack confidence in their writing ability. Several studies have shown that everyone is not entranced by technology and that interacting with a machine is not exciting for everyone. Therefore, using a computer should not be a requirement for producing business documents in business communication classes. Students should be given information and instruction whenever possible to help overcome their apprehension because they will undoubtedly need to use technology in their careers. The first objective, however, is to build confidence in the ability to write, and that can be accomplished without technology.

The appearance of "canned" business letter software is probably an attempt to help apprehensive writers. These software packages provide form letters on diskette that users can revise to suit their needs. Letters and memos dealing with granting credit, refusing adjustments, answering requests for information, following up sales contacts, and other positive, negative, and persuasive situations are provided. Experts agree that although the memos and letters in these packages are readable, they are not high-quality business messages.[5] Students, especially those who are apprehensive writers, should know the drawbacks of using such packages.

---

[4]Sterkel, Karen S.; Johnson, Mildred I.; and Sjogren, Douglas D. "Textual Analysis with Computers To Improve the Writing Skills of Business Communications Students." *Journal of Business Communication* 23:43-61; Winter 1986.

[5]Penrose, John M., Jr. "A Qualitative Comparison of Three Microcomputer Business Letter Libraries." *Journal of Business Communication* 23:23-30; Spring 1986.

Teaching students to evaluate software critically, to use simple formatting techniques, and to improve their vocabulary, grammar, and proofreading skills can help them build writing skills with technology. Teaching students to use electronic mail can help them develop another ability, assessing their writing while it is on the computer screen.

Using electronic mail. Electronic mail can be used to send memos, reports, forms, and just about any other printed message. Quite often, however, the message is never printed on paper. The user simply establishes an electronic mailbox on the system in which to receive messages. Each user has a password that prevents unauthorized access to his/her mailbox, and messages are composed on and read from the computer screen. Messages are delivered instantly and can be accessed at home, in the office, or elsewhere.

Electronic mail has increased the speed with which business communications are delivered and also the speed with which they are prepared. Consequently, poor grammar and punctuation abound in electronic mail messages because writers do little or no editing. In some cases the clarity of the message suffers as well. A positive aspect of the process is that students may improve their ability to compose messages rapidly.

Students should be encouraged to write electronic mail messages on the computer and to send them to other students. The messages should then be evaluated by the receiver for clarity and conciseness and returned to the student with suggestions for improvement. After students become familiar with the electronic mail process, teachers should insist on accurate grammar, punctuation, and spelling in electronic messages.

Students can use electronic mail to improve the mechanical accuracy of their business communications; they can also use the resources available through computer technology to improve the content of their communications.

Using electronic bulletin boards and databases for research. Electronic bulletin boards are useful both for delivering messages and for gathering information on particular topics. Electronic bulletin boards are generally menu driven, which means that users can select one operation from a list of choices. Consequently, accessing information is relatively easy and very fast.

Several national bulletin boards exist; NBEA Net, a bulletin board for business educators, is only one example of a national bulletin board that links educational communities all over the United States, including over 2,000 school districts and the state education agencies in all 50 states. Users pay a fee to subscribe to a bulletin board and are charged for transmission, connect time, and storage. Since numerous electronic information services are now available, keeping up with their offerings and costs is nearly impossible. Nevertheless, teachers can help their students become familiar with one or two. Many universities have an electronic bulletin board that faculty and students can access.

Computer databases provide substantially more information than electronic bulletin boards. In fact, they have revolutionized library research. The information explosion has inundated libraries to the extent that they cannot catalog current information fast enough for it to be timely. Computer databases are the solution to that problem. Computers are uniquely suited for not only storing but also retrieving vast amounts of data. In recent years that data has taken the form of bibliographic information. Databases similar to DIALOG, which indexes millions of documents, are being made available by vendors to the personal computer user. Students can increase the quality and quantity of their research with proper knowledge of and instruction in using databases.

A major advantage of computer or on-line databases is their currency. They are regularly updated with new information, sometimes as often as daily. A second almost equally important advantage is the speed with which users can get information. However, using a database is not a simple process. Students must learn how to use a database just as they must learn how to use the library. To do computer research, students need to know the types of databases available, what database to search, what key words to use in the search, the syntax to use for the search, and how to retrieve and/or print the desired information.

Databases can be categorized into three basic types: bibliographic databases, which give a list of references for a particular topic, usually in a particular discipline; numeric databases, which provide only data, such as stock market information; and document databases, which provide the entire document. One can choose a particular database from among hundreds within each of these categories. After choosing the database, the user enters the key word or words to find information pertaining to a particular topic. Precisely how one enters those words and proceeds through the search requires knowledge of the particular program's operation as does retrieving or printing the document.

Unless teachers have access to a database through their schools, they cannot provide hands-on instruction in database use. However, general information about using databases can be provided to students, and transparencies or handouts of typical screens of information can be shown in class and explained. Also, the common pitfalls of using databases for research should be noted. Such problems as choosing the wrong database, using the wrong search strategy, and relying on only an abstracted version of the information are common stumbling blocks. Also, databases usually do not contain information prior to 1970; therefore, library sources may need to be researched also.

In preparing a research report, students will often create graphs and charts. Computer technology offers a useful tool for this task.

Using computer technology for business graphics. Computer graphics is one area in which the microcomputer has made a significant difference in the quality of business documents. No longer does one need to be an artist or to hire an artist to produce colorful, dramatic graphs and charts for inclusion in reports and oral presentations. However, though computer graphics are attractive, they can be misleading if students are not aware of the rules for preparing graphs and charts. The result can be a decorative visual illustration that provides no clarification, causes confusion, or actually communicates the wrong message. Pfaffenberger provides three standards for producing quality graphics:

1. Tell the truth about the data.

2. Use graphics to clarify the data, not just for decoration.

3. Choose a format (line, bar, pie, etc.) that best expresses the data.[6]

Computer graphics packages can be used skillfully if these standards are kept in mind. Students should be taught the principles for preparing graphics and cautioned to use graphics packages with careful attention to those principles, especially using proportional axes and scaling the y (vertical) axis properly.

Line, bar, and column charts have an x (horizontal) axis and a y (vertical) axis. The x axis is used to show categories such as years or products. The y axis is used to show amounts or measurements, such as sales in thousands of dollars. If the axes are grossly disproportionate, the data in the graph will not be accurately represented. For example, in a line graph if the y axis is very short compared to the x axis, the data points will be elongated, thus flattening out the line; if on the other hand, the y axis is very long compared to the x axis, the data points will be elongated vertically and make the differences appear too dramatic.

Scaling the y axis properly is equally important for accurate data representation. Unequal distances between amounts on the y axis and beginning the scale with a number other than zero cause pictorial inaccuracies. For example, the columns in Figure I indicate that only half as many females compared to males enrolled in accounting classes in both 1986 and 1988 when, in fact, the data reveals that is not the case. Figure II shows an accurate representation of the data.

Male and Female Enrollments in Accounting Classes, 1986 and 1988

xxx Females
*** Males

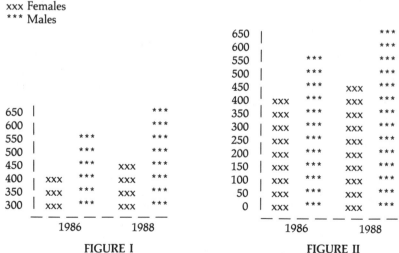

FIGURE I   FIGURE II

---

[6]Pfaffenberger, Brian. *Business Communication in the Personal Computer Age.* Homewood, Ill.: Richard D. Irwin, 1987. pp. 90-92.

Generally, technology has increased the ease of preparing written business communications; if the technology is used properly, it can also improve the appearance, accuracy, content, and overall quality of written documents.

BUILDING SPEAKING SKILLS WITH TECHNOLOGY

Technology has less impact on oral business communication today than it has on written business communication, but it may have more impact in the future. Studies suggest that business graduates will use telephone, dictation, and teleconferencing equipment, give platform speeches, and participate in business meetings more frequently in the future. In developing students' oral communication skills, teachers typically focus on the message and the delivery. Now technology has become an important part of the oral communication process. Dictation equipment can increase the speed with which correspondence is prepared, and telephone technology can facilitate everyday business transactions. Videotaping speeches can improve platform speaking skills. Finally, teleconference networks and presentation graphics can improve the quality of business meetings. However, students need to learn skills to use this technology to best advantage.

Using dictation equipment for correspondence. Dictation is not a new technology, but it is a well-known and widely used one. Businesses have accepted the fact that dictation is much more efficient than handwriting for preparing correspondence and, therefore, less expensive. Employees who prepare business documents will almost certainly have access to dictation equipment. The communication skills needed for effective dictation include oral skill: enunciation and articulation; written skill: organization, grammar, and punctuation; and technological skill: equipment operation. Many guidelines for dictation are available in the literature, and schools often have dictation equipment for students to use. Therefore, teachers can use these resources to teach dictation techniques and provide opportunities for students to practice dictating business documents.

Using telephone technology for business communications. Although telephones have been used for many years, certain telephone technology is used more by particular business people, such as sales representatives. For example, the future may see a significant increase in the use of car phones, pagers or beepers, and answering machines by people who conduct most of their business outside the office. These technologies improve the efficiency of business communications but not necessarily the effectiveness. The speed with which a message is delivered will make a difference only if the message is understood.

Many large metropolitan areas have mobile telephone services. As those services in the form of car phones and pagers become increasingly less expensive, they probably will be used more frequently by people making business contacts in the field. The use of answering machines may also increase as people attempt to avoid the telephone-tag syndrome.

Using a car phone requires the same type of communication skills as using an ordinary phone: courtesy, tact, clear message organization, and clear enunciation, to name only a few. These skills become even more critical when applied to pagers and answering machines. When an individual calls a pager or an answering machine, as little as 15 seconds may be allowed to state a message. Obviously, the inability to articulate a clear, concise message will be a serious handicap. Poorly composed and delivered messages may result in misunderstandings and wasted time at the least and could have more serious consequences.

Using videotape for oral presentations. Videotape technology has also been in use for many years and will continue to be used for oral communications. Videotaping oral presentations provides opportunities for students to analyze and improve their speaking skills. However, students should learn basic oral presentation skills before they are videotaped. Presenting a speech to a group is nerve-wracking, and having it videotaped besides can be terrifying. First, students should have the opportunity to see good speakers perform. Second, the characteristics of quality speeches should be identified and discussed. Third, students should prepare short, informal speeches for delivery to a small group. Finally, the delivery of the short speech should be analyzed by the teacher and the speaker.

After students have had some experience giving oral presentations, they can benefit from being videotaped and evaluated by their peers because they will be less intimidated by the oral presentation process. Also, they can become familiar with equipment operation by taping other students. Since videotape is one form of teleconferencing, students will also be introduced to that technology.

Using teleconferencing technology for business meetings. Teleconferencing technology can take one of several forms: speakerphones, audioconferencing, full-motion videoconferencing, or computer conferencing. Essentially, teleconferencing means some method of linking people electronically so that they can hear and/or see each other and interact as a group. The telephone conference call was an early form of teleconferencing. Electronic mail, when two or more people are linked at the same time, is a current form of teleconferencing. The teleconferencing skills that students should learn depend to some extent on the type of teleconferencing one expects them to use.

Office technology literature has promoted the view that in the near future business meetings will be conducted via video screens with audio and computer hookups to remote locations. Actually, this view has not become a reality except in very large companies. What the business graduate is more likely to encounter is some form of audioconferencing, which allows several people in various locations to hear but not to see each other.

Voice-only audioconferencing may mean several telephones linked temporarily for a conference, the conference call, or it may involve more sophisticated technologies, such as amplified speakerphones and multiple microphones, which permit a group of people at one location to participate in a meeting with other people located at different sites. Audiographic conferencing goes a step farther by allowing diagrams drawn on a writing surface at one location to be transmitted to another location where they are viewed on a screen. Cost-effective video conferencing is available, but it is limited to projection of still images only and one-way transmission. Therefore, experts believe that the electronic meeting will supplement rather than replace the traditional business meeting.[7]

Because time is an important factor in business meetings, presentations must be well organized and concise. If the participants will be heard but not seen, enunciation and articulation skills become more critical for understanding what is said. Students need to analyze and improve their voice quality, tone, volume, and pitch to use this technology well. Generally, the skills needed for videotape technology will be important also for teleconferencing. In addition, students need graphics presentation skills.

Using presentation graphics for business meetings. Presentation graphics include slides, overhead transparencies, or any other visual media that are projected on a screen. The content of the graphic may be a chart or table, but it may also be a picture or just a list of words. In any case, this type of graphic must be skillfully prepared to be effective. Some computer graphics software packages include pictures or allow the user to add text to the illustration. Some computer programs allow the user to actually draw a picture. Several rules are important in the creation of presentation graphics:

1. Be careful in using colors; colors may clash, and some people are color-blind. Colors can also have an emotional effect.

2. Seek professional help in designing a graphic or taking slides. Artistic and/or photographic training is necessary to create well-designed, clear presentations.

3. Limit the text on overhead transparencies to no more than five lines, and make the print large enough to be seen from a distance.

4. Coordinate the content of the speech with the graphics.

Students will, of course, apply written communication skills in preparing presentation graphics, but they will also need to develop coordination skill. Teachers should demonstrate how to incorporate slides and transparencies into an oral presentation, explain how to use the equipment, and allow students to practice using projection equipment while they are speaking.

CONCLUSION

Computer hardware and software as well as older technologies such as telephone, dictation, and videotape are useful business communication tools. The discriminating use of word processing software and graphics packages can help students improve their written communications; database technology can help students improve their research efforts; and sophisticated audio and video technology can help students enhance their oral communications. However, in the midst of technological advancement, teachers must keep in mind that because technology is a tool, it can be used poorly or skillfully. Therefore, teachers should help their students learn to use it skillfully so that the business communications that students produce with technology are superior to the ones they produce without it.

---

[7]Dickey, Sam. "Electronic Meetings: Substitutes with Substance?" *Today's Office* 21:41-46; July 1986.

CHAPTER 9

Increasing Communication Skills of Nonnative Speakers of English

EDWARD BEN MCCOLLOUGH

Rogers State College, Claremore, Oklahoma

A growing number of students from many other parts of the world are coming to the United States for schooling. Each year there are more nonnative students and more countries represented. Currently about 350,000 foreigners are students in American schools, a tenfold increase during the past 30 years.

International students come from widespread parts of the world. South and East Asia send by far the largest numbers of international students to the United States. Other areas in descending order of numbers of students sent to the United States for education are the Middle East, Latin America, Africa, and Europe. Malaysia, Taiwan, and Nigeria are the individual countries with the largest numbers of students studying in the United States.

The recent slump in oil prices has caused a decline in the number of students coming from countries with oil-based economies, but the number of students from other countries, particularly those in Southeast Asia, has increased. All areas of the United States have significant numbers of international students, but the states with the largest numbers of international students are California, New York, and Texas. In recent years the largest gains in international student enrollments have been in schools in the southern part of the United States.

Although engineering has long been the field of study that has attracted the largest number of foreign students, the field of business and management has gained numbers of foreign students steadily. Now the foreign student enrollment figures for engineering only slightly exceed those for business and management, although both have declined slightly in recent years.

Because large numbers of nonnative students are business and management majors and because almost all American postsecondary educational institutions require their business and management majors to complete a business communication course, postsecondary business educators should expect to teach and be prepared to teach students who are nonnative speakers of English. Because even secondary school business educators, especially those in metropolitan areas, have nonnative speakers of English as students, they, too, need to be ready to teach nonnative speakers of English. If business educators at all instructional levels are to be able to teach such students successfully, they must learn how to increase the communication skills of nonnative speakers of English—after all, communication skills are the tools that teachers use to convey subject matter and that students use to acquire subject matter.

The challenges facing teachers of business communication and other business subjects multiply as they interact with foreign students. Although deficiencies in listening, speaking, reading, and writing skills handicap many native speakers of English, they compound problems for nonnative speakers of English, who typically possess less well-developed communication skills in English. Communication-related skills in English are both the problem and the solution from the perspective of business educators. Consequently, business educators must take action to develop relevant background in order to increase the communication skills of nonnative speakers of English.

DEVELOPING THE BACKGROUND

Business educators must develop appropriate background so that they can increase the communication skills of nonnative speakers of English. Business educators must understand benefits from international student education, acquisition of language, cultural aspects of communication, language barriers to communication, and traits of successful teachers before they can implement teaching activities that build the communication skills of nonnative speakers of English.

Understanding international student education benefits. Many benefits accrue to international students, to American students, to their respective countries, and to educational institutions from having international students enroll in schools in the United States.

International students benefit from study in the United States in many ways. Since American higher education is among the best in the world, foreign students may have educational opportunities that are not available in their own countries. In addition, they may have choices of majors and freedom to select courses that are not possible at home. Foreign students may benefit from exposure to a different and sometimes more advanced culture than their own. Opportunities to develop self-reliance away from the strong family dependence found in many parts of the world may also be helpful. Furthermore, foreign students may develop a better understanding of their own countries' values and strengths and weaknesses after having lived in another country.

American students also benefit from exposure to international students. Through interaction with foreign students, American students develop a better understanding of peoples of the world and of their common characteristics and experiences; in other words, they expand from local, state, and national perspectives toward those that are global in nature. They begin to understand their own people and country through the eyes of nonnative residents. American students also benefit from exposure to other ideas and skills from abroad. They become friends with citizens of other countries, and later opportunities for travel to visit them in their native lands may develop.

Nations also benefit from the exchange of students. Many international students from developing countries later return to their homelands, becoming leaders of their countries. They are often influential in changing their societies and in developing their economies, bridging gaps between developing and developed nations. Personal ties and friendships between governmental leaders and common citizens also help to promote greater understanding and cooperation between governments. Use of English as the international language of governments and businesses is encouraged, too.

Educational institutions in the United States benefit as well. Their approaches to education broaden as they adapt to more diversified clienteles. In that process institutions are often forced to reexamine their educational philosophies, policies, and procedures. The learning environments of schools become more cosmopolitan. Foreign students enrich the education of American students and vice versa. Useful social, economic, and political relationships develop.

Understanding language acquisition. With the possible exception of some of the less developed countries, nowhere but in the United States does as much indifference exist toward learning other languages. The tales of American tourists and business people who simply raise the volume of their voices in futile attempts to make themselves understood are all too true. This has resulted in enhancing the "ugly American" image abroad. Many progressive nations require that their students devote at least several years of study to one or more other languages. Consequently, many people in other countries understand English, often speak it fluently, and are eager to practice their English language skills. In stark contrast, few Americans understand or speak another language fluently. People traveling abroad or doing business with people who speak another language are going to encounter situations where they wish for the ability to use another language.

Unfortunately for most people, their ability to learn another language easily has greatly diminished by the time they are well into their education for business. It would seem that languages are best learned by imitation and that children are, no doubt, the best imitators of sound. Differences in children's and adults' abilities to learn languages are probably caused by brain maturation. Recent research has shown that children gradually assign functions to one side of the brain or the other. Once that process is complete, typically by age 12, brains lose the flexibility necessary to acquire new languages without a great deal of effort.[1] Observation bears this out. Everyone is aware of cases where the young children of Americans living abroad have learned the local language perfectly and effortlessly, and everyone knows of families who have come to this country whose young children have learned American English easily.

International students who come to the United States after having studied English for many years can be expected to have some to little difficulty communicating. If the years of study are coupled with living in an environment where spoken English is heard, the students will have little or no difficulty in communicating in English in business or any other situations. In fact, one college recently presented its outstanding business student award

---

[1]Barnes, Gregory A. *Communication Skills for the Foreign-Born Professional.* Philadelphia: ISI Press, 1982. p. 2.

to an intelligent, hardworking young lady from Saudi Arabia, who had the added advantage of growing up in the environment of an ARAMCO compound. She spoke perfect English with hardly a trace of an accent. Her husband and two of his brothers, who had not grown up in an environment where English was spoken, had more difficulty in communicating in English.

Considering the lack of emphasis on language acquisition in the United States and the difficulties in becoming fluent in another language, are business educators wrong to expect international students coming here to be able to prepare perfect spoken and written business communications? Are business educators wrong to expect nonnative students to listen and to read at the same speeds as American students? On the surface the answers to these questions appear to be fairly obvious; business educators should not have the same expectations, but what can be done? Class standards could be adjusted downward for nonnative speakers of English to compensate for the fact that many of them will be taking their business communication knowledges and skills home with them, but is this plausible solution realistic since many nonnative speakers of English also remain in this country to work for American businesses? On second thought it appears that business educators should not adjust their standards very much—if at all—because then their business communication courses will soon lose their credibility in the business world, harming both nonnative and native speakers of English.

Understanding cultural aspects. The problems associated with increasing the communication skills of nonnative speakers of English can be lessened by better understanding of cultural aspects of communication. The better business educators and international students understand each other's cultures, the better they can work cooperatively to achieve their common goals. When members of each group are sincerely interested in knowing about the cultures of each other, the doorways to improved communication will open.

Those who have grown up in other countries frequently have many questions about American society and its culture. Because of natural biases favoring their own countries' values, attitudes, and beliefs, many international students have difficulty understanding and accepting certain aspects of American life. For example, nonnatives often express amazement at what they perceive as the lack of closeness in American families. They frequently attribute high divorce rates in the United States and juvenile crime problems to the fact that many women are employed outside their homes. Others are shocked by the freedoms Americans take for granted and by the permissiveness of American youth. Some perceive that placing aged family members in nursing homes proves that family life is destroyed in the United States.

Natives of the United States have difficulty understanding and accepting certain aspects of the cultures that nonnative students bring with them to the United States. Cultural aspects of time, space, family, and social customs are discussed to better understand communication-related behaviors of nonnative speakers of English.

Time has different degrees of importance in various cultures. Although time is relatively important in most North American and European cultures, it is of much less importance in many other cultures. While the former cultures tend to operate on mechanical time, the latter cultures tend to operate on natural time. Consequently, many foreign students think nothing of arriving late for class by 10 or more minutes; after all, that time will be used for preliminary activities, and class will still be in session when they arrive. The same attitude toward time causes many foreign students to submit their assignments to their disgruntled teachers well after the due dates and times. Because of the competitive nature of business, business educators must emphasize to those from cultures placing less value on time that it is necessary to develop a proper concept of time.

Space is perceived in various ways by those from different cultures. Americans value space, but it is also of less importance in most other cultures. Consequently, foreign students place less value on personal and living space. When most nonnative speakers of English converse among themselves, they congregate in close proximity to each other, sometimes even moving chairs within classrooms to overcrowd a row. Even when orally communicating with native speakers of English, their closeness persists, invading the personal space so valued by Americans. Perceptions about space also influence ideas about living arrangements. American landlords report that frequently foreign students want to share living quarters with large numbers of other foreigners, thus badly overcrowding the rooms by American standards.

Families are viewed differently in various cultures. Many students from foreign countries are bothered by American family life. Since such students often come from family-dependent cultures, they cannot understand the autonomy within typical American families. They sometimes perceive the lack of open affection among family members—even friends—as a sign of indifference. Since many foreign students come from cultures where the extended family is the norm, they may be surprised that most Americans do not add additional rooms to their houses to accommodate aging parents and married children and their families.

Social customs vary significantly from culture to culture. Behavior that is acceptable in one circumstance may be offensive in another or have an entirely different meaning. For example, suppose you are working at your desk when an Arab student, who is about to return to his homeland, leans over and kisses you on the forehead. How would you react? From an American cultural perspective you are likely to be embarrassed by this seemingly indecent act; from an Arabic cultural perspective, you should feel flattered since such a kiss is reserved only for those few who are held in very high respect. In the United States it is considered to be a breach of etiquette for a guest to begin eating before the host or hostess does; in the Middle East it is considered to be a breach of etiquette if the host or hostess begins to eat before a guest does. If a coffee cup is raised, extended, and moved from side to side by an American, it likely means that more coffee is desired; when the same gesture is made by a Middle Easterner, it likely means that no more coffee is desired. In all likelihood, these same behaviors have many other interpretations depending upon the cultural perspectives from which they are viewed.

Understanding language barriers. In addition to cultural barriers to communication, there are language barriers to communication as well. Many language barriers to communication can be reduced or eliminated by better understanding of words and their meanings. When native speakers of English learn about the original languages of nonnative speakers of English, many communication problems can be better understood and sometimes avoided.

American businesses have made many embarrassing and costly blunders because improper attention was given to language considerations. Some examples follow. When American Motors tried to market its American model called Matador in Puerto Rico, it did not sell well because there the word means killer. Sunbeam Corporation was puzzled why its curling iron named Mist Stick did not sell well in Germany—puzzled until it learned that mist means manure in German. Esso experienced difficulty in selling its products in Japan; later it learned that Esso means stalled car in Japanese. Free samples of Fresca were not the effective customer enticements in Mexico that they were in other countries: Shocked consumers were repulsed by the name, which is a Mexican slang term for Lesbian. Other blunders can occur when what appear to be only slight errors are made in translation from one language to another. Notice the result if the word *when* is translated as the word *until* in this sentence: Until I wore this, I felt good. In another translation incident, the word software was translated as underwear. Language barrier problems such as these are not unique to the business world; in fact they are daily occurrences in business—especially business communication—classes as native and nonnative speakers of English attempt but sometimes fail to circumvent language barriers to communication.

Language barriers are common in both oral and written communication situations. Accents and differences in pronunciations add to the problems. The vast size of the United States and the diverse backgrounds of its peoples contribute to the larger number of accents in spoken American English, accents that sometimes deviate from those found in other parts of the English-speaking world. Not only are there somewhat distinct regional differences in accents among native citizens, but also the accents vary according to the native language of those who have immigrated to the United States. Some of these differences in pronunciation can cause problems for students from abroad. Many times they will misunderstand a verb form or substitute an adjective for a noun. Their own pronunciations of English words often cause Americans to misunderstand.

Improper enunciation can cause serious embarrassment by distorting the listener's perceptions of what was said. When a middle-aged American male ordered a dozen pieces of pastry in a Viennese pastry shop, he could not understand the rather shocked reaction of the young Austrian lady who received his order or why she got a rather stern-faced older lady to complete his order, incidentally in grams, not dozens. Several years later he identified the problem: The word for dozen in German, *Duzend,* has an almost identical sound to the German verb *duzen,* which translates as to become intimately acquainted with, and he had failed to sound the final consonant. This incident illustrates what easily happens to both Americans abroad and nonnative speakers of English in the United States. Language errors, even slight ones, can create barriers to communication.

Although language errors in oral communication are heard, they tend to be even more noticeable in written communication because they are seen. Many errors in written communications prepared by nonnative speakers of English are attributable to differences in grammar from language to language. For example, most Oriental languages do not have articles; consequently, Orientals tend either to omit the words *a, an,* and *the* when writing in English or to use them unnecessarily to compensate for confusion about when they should be used. Those whose native tongues are Latin-based languages sometimes erroneously place their adjectives in English after the nouns they modify, following the practice in their native languages. Educated German-speaking people always place their past participles at the ends of their sentences in spite of their lengths; consequently, the sentence "Ich habe schön zu viel Frühstück gegessen," which literally translates as "I have already too much breakfast eaten," seems strangely ordered by English language standards.

Examples such as the ones cited in recent paragraphs reflect some of the common types of language barriers that business educators find their non-native students encountering as they attempt to communicate in English. Such mistakes are not purposely made to infuriate native speakers of English, but rather they are made out of ignorance of the many complexities of the English language. Foreign students may well wonder why some of the words are being used, for to them the sounds may mean something entirely different. Many of them are too shy, too polite, or too embarrassed to ask when they do not understand something about the English language. Consequently, business educators should encourage international students to bring and use their dictionaries during classroom activities and should actively solicit clarifying questions from them.

Most international students studying business in the United States are planning careers that include transacting business in English-speaking countries. As a result, most of them are highly motivated to improve their English language skills in order to diminish barriers to communication that might jeopardize their career plans. Although learning proper English grammar is challenging, both business educators and nonnative speakers realize how important it is to their success inside and outside of the classroom. The cultures of some international students encourage them to seek help from native speakers of English; others are more likely to try to figure it out for themselves without assistance from native speakers of English. In their zeal to learn proper English for business purposes, sometimes nonnative speakers buy, read, and study any supplementary books that they can find on business communication topics.

Understanding teaching-related traits. Business educators who teach nonnative speakers of English should cultivate and intensify those teaching-related traits that encourage and motivate international students to build their English language communication skills. Experience suggests that teachers who work best with nonnative speakers of English tend to have similar core groups of desirable teaching-related traits. While nearly everyone possesses some of these characteristics, probably very few possess all of them. The more of these desirable traits business educators possess or develop, the greater their tendencies to interact effectively with international students in educational settings. Although some business educators may have only some of these desirable teaching-related traits initially, they can take action to develop them over periods of time.

A variety of teaching-related traits comprise the desirable core group. Open-mindedness is the core trait. From it evolve awareness of and tolerance of other cultures as well as adaptability to and experience with other cultures. Curiosity about such things as world geography and facts and figures about countries and their peoples is also desirable. Interest in and ability to learn foreign languages are useful. Abilities to adjust to new conditions and to interact with a variety of people are also helpful teaching-related traits. Ideally, international students will possess similar learning-related traits.

INCREASING COMMUNICATION SKILLS

After business educators have developed relevant background so that they understand nonnative speakers of English and the problems they encounter as they try to master the English language, they are ready to begin to apply their understandings as they interact with international students in learning situations. This portion of the article does not attempt to identify or describe all of the many techniques and approaches that business educators can use to increase the English language communication skills of nonnative speakers of English. It does attempt to suggest some of the proven ways that business educators might find useful in building students' communication skills in English. A few general suggestions precede the specific suggestions relating to speaking and listening and to writing and reading.

General suggestions. Business educators should encourage interaction between native and nonnative students. One way to do this is to devise a seating plan that distributes the foreign students throughout the classroom. This approach will counter the natural tendencies of nonnative and native students to cluster with those with similar characteristics.

Business educators can also provide information to their students that builds understandings of those from other countries. This can be accomplished through oral presentations or written presentations or both. Topics such as intercultural communication are very appropriate for those who study business communication and other business specialty fields, especially when some of their classmates are foreign students. Business educators could inform students about other peoples and their countries through "Culturgrams," individual brochures available from Brigham Young University Publishing Service in Provo, Utah, that provide information about such topics as the geography and economy of some 90 different countries as well as information about such diverse subjects as appearance, gestures, greeting, eating, traveling, visiting, and shopping habits.

Business educators should select some classroom activities and assignments that are relatively culture free or that give international students opportunities to use their unique backgrounds. Often such assignments have to do with international travel or business. Such assignments are ideal for use near the beginnings of courses because they help to build the confidence of nonnatives; in fact, in some cases they may be able to assist their native-born classmates, especially when such activities are done in small groups.

Business educators can use small-group activities to build communication skills of nonnative and native speakers of English. Small-group projects force group members to communicate with each other. In that process cross-cultural communication is stimulated, and nonnative and native students typically come away with growing favorable perceptions about each other. Business educators should avoid the temptation of providing too much guidance to groups; instead they should let the group members experience communication processes and resolve their own problems if possible.

Speaking and listening suggestions. Speaking and listening skills can be built by having students visit with each other for the first few minutes of the first class period. Then ask the students to introduce each other, telling all about the other that can be remembered. After all students have made their presentations, ask the American students for questions they have about life in the countries of the foreign students. The appropriate international students respond. Then ask the foreign students to ask questions about life in the United States. Selected native-born Americans respond. This excellent get-acquainted activity spurs considerable communication among the class members, frequently more than that for which time had been allocated. It also lays the foundation for a good environment in which communication skills in the English language can be increased.

Nonnative speakers of English need many positive experiences in speaking and listening with English in a variety of circumstances to build their self-confidence. Many times international students express themselves more freely in social rather than academic settings. Although business educators can not invite all of their foreign students to their homes for dinner, they can encourage brief social conversations whenever they see nonnative speakers of English. Well-placed questions or comments by business educators about students' native lands generally serve as effective openers for conversations. By participating in events of international clubs and at international coffees, business educators can demonstrate to their foreign-born students their sincere interest in international students.

Business educators should build academic rapport with international students. As foreign students feel comfortable with their teachers, often with social rapport serving as a prelude, they will increasingly seek opinions about and assistance with their assignments. Business educators should be sure that nonnative speakers are not overlooking important points in their work because of faulty understanding of the English language. It would be appropriate, for example, for business educators to check the speech outlines of international students for topic previews, major points, and closings but not for the detailed phrasing of ideas. Business educators could indicate that some or specific ideas need to be rephrased because of language usage errors, but they should encourage nonnative speakers to locate and correct their own errors. Many schools have learning centers that offer international students and others excellent tutorial and supplementary assistance beyond the scope of that which business educators can reasonably be expected to provide.

Writing and reading suggestions. Writing and reading skills can be strengthened by having students write and then critique each other's letters. This activity also builds empathy among senders and receivers because they begin to understand some of the many factors that influence communication. Since the English language classes that foreign students take in their countries often emphasize oral communication rather than written communication, native speakers of English may be shocked by the elementary—often incorrect—sentence constructions of nonnatives; while they know that native speakers of English may be struggling with the sometimes confusing rules of written English, they quickly understand how potentially devastating it must be for foreign students to try to write correctly in English.

As business educators and their students learn more about each other's languages, they will be better able to minimize communication problems. Empathy toward writers and readers can also be emphasized by having firsthand experiences in translating documents from one language to another. Figure I shows a short business letter written in German, an abbreviated German/English dictionary, and an English translation of the German letter. Students are asked to translate the German letter into correct American business English using the word definitions given in the dictionary. After they finish, they may see the English translation of the German letter. Although this activity seems simple on the surface, students will soon discover otherwise because of a variety of barriers to communication. Consequently, American students will have greater understanding of the complexities of communicating in another language and will be willing to assist international students as they work on assignments in the English language. A variation of this activity is to have foreign students translate the English version of the letter into their native languages and then ask other students from their countries to translate the letters into English.

Business educators can have both nonnative and native speakers of English explain meanings of well-known proverbs in writing. After the explanations are written, students exchange and then read them. If international students have misunderstood the proverbs, then American students orally explain them. This interesting exercise is a good one because it typically involves the participants' using their reading, writing, speaking, and listening skills. Proverbs such as "A stitch in time saves nine," "The early bird gets the worm," "One man's meat is another man's poison," and "Strike while the iron is hot" are useful ones for this activity. Slang expressions, such as "I was pea green with envy," "They always try to keep up with the Joneses," and "Put that in your pipe and smoke it" can be substituted for proverbs.

Business educators can assign topics of an international nature for research- and report-writing assignments. This approach broadens the typically narrow backgrounds of American students by exposing them to unfamiliar topics and allows foreign students to prepare assignments relating to familiar topics

FIGURE I. Letter Translation Exercise

German Letter

Johann Ebert
Hamburg
Kantstrasse 18
Hamburg, den 5. März 1988
Verlag Franz Müller
Berlin
Bismarkstrasse 25

In dem Briefumschlag übersende ich Ihnen einen Scheck für DM30, für zwei Jahresabonnemente zu Ihrer Zeitschrift, Der Spiegel.

Hochachtungsvoll!

Johann Ebert

Johann Ebert

German/English Dictionary

Abonnemente	subscription	Jahres	year
Briefumschlag	envelope	März	March
dem, den	the, that, which, who	Scheck	check
ein, einen	a, an, one, someone	Strasse	street
für	for	übersenden	to send, forward,
hochachtungsvoll	yours faithfully		dispatch
ich	I, self	Verlag	publishing house
Ihnen	you	Zeitschrift	periodical, magazine
Ihrer	your	zu	to, toward(s)
in	in, into	zwei	two

American Business English Translation

18 Kant Street
Hamburg, West Germany
March 5, 1988

Franz Mueller (Miller) Publishing House (Company)
25 Bismark Street
Berlin, West Germany

Ladies and Gentlemen:

Enclosed in the envelope find a check for 30 marks for two years' subscription to your magazine, *Der Spiegel.*

Very truly yours,

Johann Ebert

Johann Ebert

with which they feel comfortable. Possible topic areas include facets of trade, economics, travel, and others.

CONCLUSION

Business educators can increase the communication skills of nonnative speakers of English. Before they attempt to do so, they need to understand the many factors that influence the development of language skills. Then business educators, mindful of what they have learned about building language skills, can use appropriate methods and techniques in their business classes to increase the communication skills of nonnative speakers of English.

CHAPTER 10

Developing Intercultural Communication Skills
For the Global Business Community

ADELINA M. GOMEZ
University of Colorado, Colorado Springs

Recently a newspaper carried a story about an Asian being refused a loan by his American banker to open a family-operated business. Normally this common occurrence would hardly merit space in many newspapers simply because banks probably turn down several loans in one business day alone. What makes this a newsworthy story is the conflict of cultural values and the subsequent breakdown in communication that occurred between the banker and the Asian. As the news story described the situation, the Asian had listed an unrealistic (by American standards) income in completing the loan application. How could a man who worked for minimum wage report an hourly rate of $24.50, the bank asked. The response was simple: It was what the family—father, mother, three sons, one daughter, one brother— earned per hour. The Asian argued the legitimacy of the application and the honor of the family. The banker argued the legality of the transaction and the policies of the bank. It is obvious neither party sufficiently understood the diverse cultural patterns, behaviors, and business practices of the other culture. They were communicating from two distinct and different perspectives.

Now consider the following situation as reported in *Intercultural Communication*, a text by Samovar and Porter.

Mr. S, a highly recommended, highly motivated, and task-oriented American executive, has accepted a position as an advisor in a Third World country. While there, he will be working directly with Mr. Akwagara, a national who has the same qualifications in his own country as S has in the United States.

Within a few weeks Mr. S has begun to experience considerable frustration. It seems to him that Mr. Akwagara and his subordinates are inefficient and unmotivated. He has even attempted, in a tactful manner, to suggest to him that his work is inefficient and ineffective, but Akwagara's responses seem to S to indicate total indifference. Thinking that in an informal setting he may be more successful in making Akwagara aware of the problems, S suggests that the two go out for a few drinks. It didn't work; each time S tried to bring up the work situation, Akwagara changed the subject to unrelated chatter about family and friends.

The problem became increasingly severe in the weeks that followed. So to S, the only recourse was to do most of the work himself. Gradually he assumed more responsibilities without Akwagara's consent, and while he is concerned, he knows he is getting the job done which he was sent to do.[1]

The consequences of this situation are serious enough to create major cross-cultural problems. Mr. S has been successful in transferring his American job-related skills to the host culture, but he may have inadvertently caused Mr. Akwagara to lose face among his own people. Additionally, Mr. Akwagara may have formed some strong opinions that substantiate, for him, the belief of the "ugly American." What is lacking here is appropriate training in cultural differences and in intercultural communication for Mr. S, as he is the one entering a new culture.

These scenarios are played out many times over, leaving the participants either unaware that cultural norms have been violated or frustrated because they don't understand or know enough about each other's behaviors to interact effectively. The following pages, then, represent an attempt to define intercultural communication and identify useful skills for interacting more effectively with other cultures by describing how business educators can prepare their students to be effective participants in the global business community.

WHAT IS INTERCULTURAL COMMUNICATION?

Intercultural communication began when mankind first engaged in trade, wars, exploration, and colonization. Although it was not necessarily labeled communication, the interaction among different groups of people necessitated some form of communication. Through the years, at its best, intercultural communication has been ineffective. Until recently, it occurred primarily within relatively small groups. Representatives of government, heads of state, and other privileged and designated groups traveled into other cultures and interacted with their counterparts, usually for political or business reasons.

In the United States interactions among the cultural or ethnic groups have increased only within the last 20 years. The macroculture, the Anglo-culture, was usually distinctly separated from the microcultures. The inhabitants of the ghettos and barrios remained predominantly in those environs—leaving only to work in the macroculture, with only a handful of them able to interact as equals.

Numerous occurrences in the last two decades have been credited with creating an awareness and a need for a clearer understanding of what intercultural communication should be. One of those was the enactment of the civil rights bill in the 1960's; it is the impetus that helped focus on the importance of effective communication among culturally diverse groups. In addition, improved methods of transportation made travel to other countries easier; and where middle class Americans had only dreamed of travel to distant lands, now it had become a reality. Not only were American businesses and corporations becoming interested in establishing plants and offices abroad, but Europeans and Orientals were expressing similar interests

---

[1]Samovar, Larry A., and Porter, Robert E. *Intercultural Communication: A Reader.* Third edition. Belmont, Calif.: Wadsworth Publishing Co., 1982. pp. 235-36.

in the United States. Finally, it was a general awakening to the realities of life that people representing different cultures were, in many respects, different from one another and were likely to stay that way. It became evident that the need was to develop a global viewpoint that would focus on, among other things, awareness of common goals and aspirations as well as respect for different value systems of other cultures. It also became necessary to develop in people the knowledge, skills, and attitudes needed to live effectively in a world characterized by ethnic diversity, cultural pluralism, and increasing interdependence.

In developing intercultural communication skills, it is helpful to analyze the role of sender and receiver in sending and receiving verbal and nonverbal messages. Experts have argued that communication is more effective when the two individuals sending and/or receiving messages have similar fields of experience; for example, their beliefs, attitudes, and values, as well as other factors, parallel each other's. The basic premise is that there is not as much interference in the process of communication because the participants' perceptions and interpretations are similar. This means that few barriers exist; therefore, communication between the two is effective and productive. Of course, even when there are similarities, problems still exist because of the many variables that are not readily recognized. Although the participants in the communication experience are using the same language, each is responsible for determining whether the other understood the message as it was intended. This is where communication can begin to break down because of differences in communication styles, particularly in language usage. Often, the participants forget that meaning of language lies within the person who will determine what meaning to attribute to the words received. Other variables affecting the communication process include the evaluations of the sender by the receiver and vice versa, the noise or distortion factor, and the perception of self. There are, of course, many other variables affecting the process.

Intercultural communication education focuses on what happens to the message when the participants are from different cultural backgrounds. It emphasizes the argument that effective communication skills can be developed when all the different variables influencing the communication process are understood. A goal of intercultural communication education is to point out the pitfalls and the problems in the communication process between persons of different cultural backgrounds. That is why in a course of study there is an attempt to stress the roles that self-perception, perception of others, behavior of self, and behavior of others play in the communication process.

From the perspective of self-perception, students learn about beliefs, values, and attitudes that are directly attributed to the culture in which each is born. For example, attitudes begin to form early on the basis of each person's values and beliefs. Often attitudes vary in intensity with the more intense ones being more difficult to change than the less intense. One attitude that interferes with effective intercultural communication is called ethnocentrism. This has been defined as the tendency to view others and their cultures from the perspective of an individual's own culture and then judge them accordingly.

Through ethnocentric behaviors, stereotypes of others are formed, especially when others' behaviors are radically different.

WHAT BUSINESS EDUCATORS CAN TEACH THEIR STUDENTS ABOUT INTERCULTURAL COMMUNICATION

Cross-cultural interaction today is inevitable whether it is for business or for pleasure. For example, in school, in the workplace, and in recreational activities, people are brought together for many reasons. These people often represent various cultural backgrounds. Schools are often the place where much of this cross-cultural interaction takes place. Teachers of business courses can help improve cross-cultural understanding by being the catalysts for developing awareness in their students about the need for and the usefulness of knowing about others whose beliefs, values, and attitudes are different from their own. The end results could yield effective skills that will help them be better informed and aware students, consumers, or employees, as well as more empathetic and sensitive to cultural differences.

The following suggestions for classroom activities are not definitive, but they are useful as learning tools in understanding cultural differences and/or similarities. They can be modified to suit the need and the course of study. They may be added to units of study or may be used independently. The teacher can expand them or modify them in other ways.

American culture. A useful exercise is one that focuses on some of the cultural values of the American people. It can help students begin to understand what values Americans carry with them in work or in recreational activities, why they behave as they do, and why other cultures behave differently. The exercise can be incorporated into a unit on consumerism or into a discussion on American products and what they represent or why people buy them.

Introduce the exercise by discussing with the class the products that they or their parents buy that are considered typically American products, products that do not have an origin in another culture. Ask them to name some of them; if they are stymied, suggest to them that the tea bag, although now available in other countries, was first introduced in this country. Although tea is a common beverage in this country, it is consumed in larger quantities in other countries like Great Britain, Japan, and India. It is usually prepared and served more ceremoniously and with much more time. While Americans may drink large quantities of tea, it is rarely in the same manner as in other cultures. In fact, Americans have created instant teas, decaffeinated teas, and other sundry teas. The tea bag is usually considered to be a time-saver as are the instant teas—people can satisfy their urge for a cup of tea without having to spend too much time preparing it.

Continuing the discussion, the teacher can invite the students to talk about the significance or purpose of the tea bag. An introductory question is, How long does it take to brew a cup of tea when you use a tea bag? The expected and desired response is "a few minutes." That leads into a discussion on how important time is for the American culture. This view of time is quite different from that of many other cultures; Americans view and use time as if it were a tangible item. They "give" someone a few minutes. They "waste" time. They "borrow" or "take" a few minutes of someone's time. They even "spend" or "save" it. Someone from another culture once observed that she compared the practice of daylight saving time in this country to someone cutting the bottom part from a blanket and then sewing it to the top part to make it longer. She explained that she could not understand the concept of saving time involved in this practice.

Within the United States there are cultural differences related to the view and use of time. For instance, native Americans' concept of time often varies from others', so much so that their languages often do not have words for late or waiting. Individuals learn about time and use time according to their culture, and their cultural values are often reflected in their time orientations.

There are two variations to this assignment. First, the assignment can relate to items or products that are typically American and that demonstrate the culture's time orientation. Second, it can focus on items or products that demonstrate other values of the American culture, the value of the work ethic, ingenuity, and so on. Once the students understand the goal of the assignment, it can be explained that this is a way to learn about who they are, if they are American, and why they act and react as they do. The teacher can proceed with the assignment by having the students learn as much as they can about the product or item they have chosen and then talk to the class for three to five minutes about the item's significance to American culture.

Since there is always the probability of duplication of items, an alternative is to have a list of items, one for each student. Other items besides the tea bag include the cowboy hat, the electric light, the telephone, Levis or blue denim work pants, and so on. If there are students who represent other cultures, they should be encouraged to bring an item from their culture and discuss its cultural relevance. This then becomes an even greater cross-cultural learning experience.

Proverbs and superstitions. Important cross-cultural values are the concepts of individualism versus team or group orientation. Some cultures, especially the American, stress the importance of individual effort, while others stress the importance of working for or with a group such as the family or the organization. The cultural behavior from the latter perspective gives primary emphasis to the group or group needs; the individual's significance lies mainly within the context of the group. Some cultures where this is so are the Oriental, Russian, and Latin American ones. On the other hand, individualism, an American value, begins for a person at a very early age. The child in this culture develops a unique perspective for understanding his/her world that is not necessarily the perspective developed by, for example, the Russian or Oriental child.

The American perspective is often described as individuality. From this perspective, the child learns the importance of the self; self-centeredness (not necessarily a derogatory term) becomes a behavior that Americans develop. They learn early to question things, develop their own opinions, make their own decisions, and solve their own problems. Other cultures, where this is not the norm, may perceive this behavior as a form of disrespect for authority. This can often create misunderstandings between business associates who are from two culturally diverse groups.

When people develop a better understanding of intercultural differences, they begin to strengthen their communication skills. Oftentimes cross-cultural understanding can come from insignificant and seldom-thought-of-ways. Consider the following proverbs or maxims that demonstrate the cultural values of individualism and group orientation. The American proverb is "The early bird gets the worm"; the Japanese proverb translated into English is "The nail that sticks out is soon hammered down." The latter, it is said, is posted in many Japanese classrooms.

A useful exercise is to ask students for proverbs that they have heard their parents or grandparents recite. Sometimes they have been used in conjunction with an event or occasion; for instance, vacillation by one family member may prompt another to say, "He who hesitates is lost." Be forewarned, though, that only a few students will know any proverbs. The alternative, then, is for the instructor to compile a list of proverbs that are considered American and to gather some others that originated in other cultures. An interesting discussion can be generated by the students' interpretations of the proverbs and what they learn about themselves as Americans and about other cultures. Other points to ponder include whether other cultures would derive the same meanings as Americans or whether they would be offended. For example, how would the saying "beggars can't be choosers" be interpreted in India?

The same procedure is recommended for superstitious beliefs. It is safe to assume that almost everyone has a superstition that influences his/her behavior even though minimally. In other cultures superstitions—at least by American perceptions—may guide the lives of their people. In India, for example, when a child is born, certain individuals may be consulted by the child's parents so that the astrological signs will be studied along with the signs of another child and a union of marriage can be planned for the two in 15 or 20 years.

The goal of the exercise can be to discuss whether students have begun to grasp an understanding of the difficulties of communication when there is little knowledge of the other person's culture. The instructor can explain that this lack of knowledge is never as crucial as in business transactions between Americans and another culture's representatives. The consequences may mean the successful completion of a business transaction worth millions of dollars or the break-off of what might have been a mutually successful business relationship. The businessman or businesswoman who is aware of cultural differences in behaviors is going to be much more successful in his/her work when it means interacting with representatives of other cultures.

Community resources. Often overlooked resources within the community are businessmen, foreign exchange students, colleagues, and any other individuals with solid experience in interacting with other cultures or who are members of other cultures. It is useful to establish a pool of volunteer speakers who will serve as transmitters of their cultures through their presentations. Speakers can be found in often overlooked places. For example, are there any ex-Peace Corps volunteers within the community? What about German or Oriental women married to American men, or American women married to men from other cultures? Is there an international club for foreign students at the local college or university? Are there fellow teachers within the school who represent minority cultures? The wealth of information related to cross-cultural differences that these people can provide can often supersede any textbook information.

A newspaper story reported that a Japanese businessman working in the United States also is teaching American businessmen to speak Japanese at their own request. In a speech on Japanese and American business relations, he revealed to his audience that it is commendable that Americans are motivated to learn the Japanese language. But he cautioned that merely learning to speak the language is not enough; Americans must be aware of *how* to speak it as well. The point he made is that English is a forceful and direct language and that Americans are accustomed to behaving accordingly, while the Japanese language is less forceful and direct.

A guest speaker can contribute much to the understanding of and development of intercultural communication skills. The audience learns about the speaker's culture, about barriers that have developed because of ignorance of cultural differences, what types of experiences have led to misunderstandings, and what perceptions he/she had of Americans previously and now. Some of the best learning often comes from learning about the experiences of others. Most people are very willing to share their views with those who want to know about cultural differences. If there is the opportunity to have an ethnic minority person as a speaker, there are at least two questions that often produce much discussion: What misconceptions do people have about the speaker's minority group, and what misconceptions does the minority member have concerning members of other ethnic groups or concerning members of the dominant culture?

Another way to develop this exercise is to ask students to interview someone from another culture by asking questions relevant to the development of intercultural communication skills and then to write a report on their findings. This assignment combines two kinds of learning for the student: learning about cultural differences and learning effective report writing skills. Not to be overlooked in the process is the learning of interviewing skills.

Economics and intercultural communication. Economics is one of those words that brings a chill to many a student's spine, particularly when it refers to the course of study. Yet, in reality, economics is a useful business course because, as Leonard Silk said, "The range of economics is astonishing: it reaches from the prosaic daily business of the marketplace and the factory to the great philosophical issues of human welfare, freedom, and equality— from the price of beans to the price of life."[2] What better business course than economics to learn about cross-cultural differences. Students can be assigned to choose a specific culture for the purpose of researching a

---

[2]Silk, Leonard. *Economics in Plain English.* New York: Simon & Schuster, 1979. p. 171.

dimension of its economy and then comparing it to the equivalent dimension in the United States. This kind of exercise involves the student in a variety of activities that turn into learning experiences about his/her culture and about another culture that might be very diverse or similar to the American culture.

Some of the economics-related dimensions of any given culture include that culture's prime industry. Is the culture primarily agrarian? industrial? Are the people seafarers? Learning about the economics of the culture can lead to some understanding of its people. An assignment of this kind can be likened to putting together a giant jigsaw puzzle; students accumulate many pieces and then put them together to get a clearer picture of the culture and its people.

Suppose a student decides to study the food buying habits of the people. In some East Asian cultures, it is the practice of the people to buy their food on a daily basis; Americans usually shop on a weekly basis. Questions for discussion can be, How would the practice of daily grocery shopping affect the American economy, and what adjustments have East Asians had to make in their shopping habits since immigrating to this country? The discussion on these issues could extend into "what ifs." What if Americans changed their food buying habits? What impact would that have on the American economy? How many different grocery-related businesses would that affect? Would that eliminate the need for refrigeration? Why/why not? What would happen to the production of perishable goods such as frozen food items? The obvious response will surely be that it would never happen here, but the lesson to be learned is that other cultures' needs, economically speaking, are different and that they have a direct influence on the values, beliefs, and attitudes of their people. A refrigerator-freezer may be more of a luxury than a necessity, or even a useless item if people have no electricity.

Another assignment or exercise is to compare standards of living between cultures with the goal being to determine the basis of economic indicators for the countries or cultures being compared. Many students respond with enthusiasm and lively discussion when men's and women's jobs and incomes are used as comparisons. Most have a general knowledge of American men's and women's jobs and incomes, but how many know that in Peru and Canada there is an equal representation of males and females in government offices and jobs, and that in Saudi Arabia women make up less than 20 percent of university teachers but almost 100 percent of primary school teachers? Not many may know that women represent about one-third of the paid labor force worldwide, or what kinds of work women from other cultures are involved in and whether they are married or single. For example, in some Middle East cultures, there are strong constraints against married women working or even being too active outside their homes, which places them in a very different position than American women. The cross-cultural learning from this last example gives students a stronger awareness of the differences among women of various cultures and how these differences influence the perceptions people will have of one another. Lack of understanding will develop communication barriers; learning will eliminate the barriers.

Basic business and intercultural communication. The following exercise to help students learn about others can be implemented in a basic business class. It is a lesson based on questions that students answer from the research that they will conduct about another country. Here are the questions:

1. In the country of your choice, is the price asked for merchandise fixed or are customers expected to bargain? How is the bargaining conducted?
2. If as a customer you touch or handle merchandise for sale, will the storekeeper think you are knowledgeable? inconsiderate? within your rights? completely outside your rights? other?
3. How do people organize their daily activities? What are their work and meal schedules? Is there a daytime rest period? How does this affect the work schedule?
4. How does the normal work schedule accommodate environmental conditions such as the heat or the cold?
5. How will your financial position and living conditions compare with those of the majority of people living in this country?
6. What is the history of the relationships between this country and the U.S.?
7. Is education in this country free and/or compulsory?
8. How long is the school year and school day?
9. What kinds of schools are considered best: public, private, or religious?
10. Are school children integrated or segregated? If segregated, is it by race, by class, by caste, or by sex?
11. Are school children expected to work? If so, at what age and for how many hours?
12. What are the important holidays? How are they observed?
13. What are the favorite leisure and recreational activities of teenagers and/or of adults?
14. What sports are popular?
15. What kinds of television programs are shown and for what purposes? Are they instructional or entertaining?

Undoubtedly, the instructor can add several more questions that reflect the purpose or goal of the course and that will still focus on cross-cultural understanding. Answers to the questions give students further insights into how others live and why they act as they do.

Group projects. The following group projects have proved successful if students are given ample time and guidance with periodic checks to ensure successful presentations. The first project for a group of five to six students, with the number of groups per class being determined by the number of students enrolled, necessitates each group selecting a particular country or culture. In fact, it would be all right if one of the groups selected the culture of the United States, or even one of the ethnic cultures within the United States. Once the selection is made, the following steps explain the assignment. Each group member assumes the responsibility of searching for information about a specific characteristic of that culture. Characteristics or dimensions of cultures can include the nonverbal communication styles; these are divided into such categories as gestures (the meanings to gestures are not universal—

they vary from culture to culture) or hand movements and signs. The gesture for "okay" in the Western cultures is made by forming a circle with the index finger and the thumb, while in Laos the same gesture would be interpreted as a meaning for bad or nothing; in Japan it is a signal for money.

Another dimension of nonverbal communication that can vary from culture to culture is eye contact. One of the rules of eye contact, at least in the Western culture, is that the listener maintain eye contact with the speaker; if the person being spoken to looks away, this behavior may be interpreted by the speaker as a sign of boredom, disinterest, or disrespect. In other cultures, the native American ones, for example, the opposite is true. Not to look the speaker in the eye is considered paying respect to that person.

The use of space is part of nonverbal communication. The way people use space sends a message to the person perceiving the behavior. In Western cultures, people value their personal space and feel uncomfortable when people whom they do not know well move into that private space. It has been reported that American businessmen have felt uncomfortable around Saudi Arabian businessmen and have called them "pushy" because they communicate "too close." Middle Easterners, on the other hand, often perceive Westerners as "cold" and "distant." Middle Eastern cultures are accustomed to communicating with others almost nose to nose. When neither culture is aware of each other's behaviors, misperceptions develop, stereotypes are formed, and miscommunication occurs.

While nonverbal communication research is very popular with students, there are other characteristics of cultures that are just as useful for understanding cultural differences. Learning about the family unit in any culture is important. Studying how people live can yield such information as whether they have nuclear or extended family life-styles. The nuclear family is the one that is established independent of other family members; for example, a newlywed couple who move out of and away from their families' homes is a nuclear family. On the other hand, the extended family unit is one where three, and sometimes four, generations live together, and all contribute in some way to the day-to-day activities of the family. In the extended families, the elderly may have an important role within the family and are usually highly respected for their wisdom.

Other dimensions of cultures for students to research include the political structures; the laws which people abide by; the educational systems; the influences of religions; the social customs such as dating practices, marriage ceremonies, death rites and/or rituals; and the dietary and eating habits with an emphasis on what the staple foods of the culture are. Another important dimension of any culture is its health and medical services.

After students have compiled their information, the teacher schedules the group presentations. It is useful to allow 20 to 30 minutes for each group presentation. The discussion time with other class members may be in addition to that time-frame recommendation.

A variation of the assignment is that instead of a panel discussion format, the groups develop the assignment, using the same criteria, into a training program. The group members become trainers, and their goal is to develop a training program from the information they have gathered. The purpose is to train individuals to integrate successfully into the other culture without suffering from cultural shock. The purpose of this exercise is to help the students learn what it takes to communicate successfully with someone who may be minimally or considerably different from them. Learning about others and their beliefs, attitudes, values, and behaviors minimizes the difficulties in communicating. Sometimes not knowing the language that someone else speaks is the least of the problems if there is genuine and empathetic understanding.

This and other exercises described in the previous pages can be useful for helping students develop effective intercultural communication skills. The exercises are intended as suggestions for business educators whose creativity will lead them to develop additional ones that more closely address the course content of their business classes. It is through sensitivity to cultural differences that business educators can help their students become better communicators.

CONCLUSION

Many factors have necessitated educators taking a major role in preparing their students to live, work, and play in a multicultural environment. One factor is the realization of the importance of effective communication among all peoples. It has become clear that there is very little that anyone does that is not influenced or affected by communication; yet it is the very core of where most have difficulties being effective. It is said that communication is more effective when there are similarities between the participants in the communicative act. There was a time when people interacted primarily with those whose cultural backgrounds were similar to their own and when no one paid much attention to the role of communication because everyone seemed to get along just fine. Within the last 20 years social change, social progress, and strong awareness have dictated numerous changes in societies.

The "global village" concept, which is used to describe the accessibility to other countries and/or cultures, has become a major factor for all educators. For one thing, it has become apparent that even within the boundaries of the United States, equal rights did not necessarily have the same meaning for all concerned. Communication was ineffective, to say the least, and much misunderstanding, confusion, and even unrest began to develop.

Attention has now turned toward the importance of interacting satisfactorily with people at home and abroad. Although multinational organizations have relied heavily on their personnel being effective in cross-cultural business transactions, there have been too many frustrations for all concerned.

Business educators, then, can modify their business curriculums and include relevant exercises that demonstrate the problems that often arise through a lack of understanding of the behaviors of others who may be culturally different. It is the responsibility of educators to expand the visions of their students by helping them develop the knowledges and skills that will make them more effective communicators in the global business community.

Part IV

APPLICATIONS: CURRICULUMS AND METHODOLOGIES

CHAPTER 11

Teaching Communication for Business
At the Secondary Level

SUSAN MAXAM

Eastern High School, Lansing, Michigan

Communication skills, or lack of them, are always mentioned as a priority item whenever business educators talk with business people, advisory boards, or other interested community people concerning the needs of high school students. Business leaders are concerned that as larger numbers of people are employed in information-related jobs, fewer new graduates can follow simple directions, listen and respond to oral and written inquiries, or edit and make corrections to simple business documents. Employers indicate that the top three technical communication skills needed by employees are spelling, punctuation, and grammar skills, followed by other skills such as computer experience, typewriting, shorthand, and accounting. While these technical skills are priority concerns, business people now stress the critical need for employees who can actively listen, understand, and follow directions. Employees need these basic and technical communication skills in order for their employing companies to be competitive in today's information society, especially since they use communication skills approximately 70 percent of their workdays. With every function in the business world relating to or depending upon some form of communication, the level of communication skills demanded is becoming even more technical. Since employees with good communication skills are valued assets, educators—especially business educators—are challenged to educate students in all phases of written and oral communications.

How can business educators meet this pressing challenge for students with better communication skills and still have time to teach the critical job skills for entry-level office positions, general business knowledges, and economic concepts? The challenge for business educators is how to incorporate communication skills throughout the business curriculum in meaningful ways. Then students completing business programs can be competitive in the job market by filling the critical need for employees with good communication skills.

Since business educators must place more emphasis on communication skills, they should use two major approaches to develop the basic communication skills of their students. First, business educators should offer specialty courses in business English/communication that build on communication skills learned in elementary and middle schools, provide necessary remedial work in basic English language skills, and strengthen written and oral communication skills. Second, business educators should integrate communication skills into courses for and about business so that listening, speaking, reading, and writing are stressed. By building the communication skills of students in every business class, business educators can strengthen their vocational and basic business education programs as well.

TEACHING COMMUNICATION SKILLS
THROUGH SPECIALTY COURSES

Business educators should offer one or more specialty courses in business English/communication in high schools to help secondary students develop their communications skills for business. What the course is called—Business English, Business Correspondence/Writing, or Business Communication—is of less concern. Business English courses typically emphasize English language skills and the preparation of simple written communications. Business correspondence/writing courses typically place less emphasis on English language skills and more emphasis on preparing a variety of written communications. Business communication courses typically deal with communication in a broader context than do the other courses. Although the various classes tend to stress somewhat different combinations of communication skills, any such course helps to develop students' listening, speaking, reading, and writing skills.

Typical content. While the scope and content of business English/communication courses at the high school level vary depending upon the school, teacher, and textbook used, the main objective of these courses is, according to Waters and Leonard in Delta Pi Epsilon's Rapid Reader No. 6 titled *Teaching Business Communication*, "to develop proficiency in conducting business effectively through written and oral communications."[1] Incidentally, this publication provides an excellent overview of possible content as well as instructional strategies, assignment types, and evaluation procedures for such courses.

BUSINESS ENGLISH. Beginning with a thorough review of English essentials, the business English course typically involves concentrated study of the following types of units: parts of speech and their usage; word choice and sentence structure; common punctuation marks; special punctuation marks; agreement and parallelism in sentences; capitalization, abbreviations, and number style; and words and word reference/usage. While a full semester could be spent on the review of English essentials alone, many business educators introduce a business writing style unit to keep students' interest after several weeks of concentrated basic English skills study. Effective word choice is introduced and followed by practice in writing well-structured sentences; then logical paragraph organization is developed. Finally, students learn how to write business documents. Often oral communication skills receive little or no stress in the business English course.

---

[1]Waters, Max L., and Leonard, Don. *Teaching Business Communications.* Delta Pi Epsilon Rapid Reader No. 6. St. Peter, Minn.: Delta Pi Epsilon, 1985. p. 1.

BUSINESS CORRESPONDENCE/WRITING. The Business correspondence/writing course typically gives somewhat equal stress to both English language skills and the preparation of such common types of written business communications as letters and reports. Among common units of instruction are language usage; business correspondence writing style; written business communication principles, including the *you* attitude and the *seven C's* —courtesy, consideration, clarity, correctness, completeness, conciseness, and concreteness; organizational guidelines; content guidelines; and format guidelines. Oral communication activities typically receive limited stress in the business correspondence/writing course.

BUSINESS COMMUNICATION. In the business communication course, students typically are exposed to business communication in a broader context than in either business English or business correspondence/writing. Communication is presented as interaction between senders and receivers. The English language becomes a tool for both written and oral communication. Although the course typically covers the usual topics relating to language usage and written communications, it also includes aspects of oral communication as well. Among these are interpersonal communication, group communication, and unofficial or grapevine communication. Nonverbal communication through such things as body posture, facial expressions, and even clothing can also be included.

No matter which course is offered—Business English, Business Correspondence/Writing, or Business Communication—it can improve students' written and oral communication skills. With more people handling information, business educators need to accept the challenge of improving the reading, listening, speaking, and writing skills of their students. Any of the business English/communication courses will help strengthen students' basic English skills and demonstrate the importance of considering the receiver of the communication. In addition, any of the courses will emphasize that written and oral communications need to be correct in grammar, punctuation, presentation, and the like. By practicing both written and spoken communication skills in such courses, students increase their potential for effective communication with others in the workplace.

Since students develop basic language arts skills in any business English/communication course, they should receive high school English credit for it. By enrolling in a business English/communication course, students receive an intensive review of basic language arts essentials and an introduction to business document writing—both aspects of communication that the increased graduation requirements in English seek to improve. The Wisconsin Department of Public Instruction, for example, gives an English credit for one semester of business communication or shorthand study, according to Condon and Schlattman, because both courses provide students with the basic English skills that society and employers are demanding.[2] Business educators elsewhere should take action to ensure that their students receive similar credit toward high school graduation. By offering one or more specialty courses

[2]Condon, Gregg, and Schlattman, Ronald. "Business Education on the Offensive—Alternative English Credit." *Business Education Forum* 40:6-9; February 1986.

105

in business English/communication, business educators can provide their students with both the technical communication skills needed in the information society and English credit toward graduation.

Instructional strategies. A wide array of teaching strategies are available for business educators to use in teaching business English/communication courses. As business educators present the course content, they should structure their students' learning activities to build good listening, speaking, reading, and writing skills and to develop acquaintanceship with electronic media communication applications.

LISTENING. Listening skills should be introduced early in the course and then reinforced throughout the semester. Oral directions can be given to students daily with reminders to concentrate on what is actually being said, raise necessary questions when appropriate, and respond appropriately to the directions. This may help to diminish employers' concern that graduates cannot follow simple directions. Business educators can also discuss oral communication models and skills and then reinforce these skills daily when giving directions for other lessons. If students learn these listening skills early, the rest of the course will be easier because students will know how to listen to the teacher's instructions, ask clarifying questions, and respond to directions. Another important listening skill involves hearing a speech or discussion and identifying its major points. Students should have opportunities to listen to oral presentations and then analyze the audience and the presentation content, technique, and effectiveness. Many excellent cassette tapes on listening skills are available to business educators for classroom use.

SPEAKING. Practice in giving directions allows students to focus on speaking skills. Students can plan directions, organize their thoughts so that the directions are complete, clear, and precise, and sequence the supporting details. Topics can range from how to insert paper into the typewriter to how to get to the nearest bank to cash a check. Students quickly learn that organization is a key factor in any communication and that the method of communication chosen will depend upon the audience and the purpose of the communication.

Other interesting oral exercises can build good spoken communications while developing technical communication skills. Holder's students write introductions of each other and then give the introductions orally during the first week of the course.[3] Students make decisions on what questions need to be asked and then organize the writing of their introductions around the audience. In an exercise suggested by Burtness and Hulbert, students discover the importance of different words in the sentence depending upon the intent of the speaker.[4] Each student reads a sentence in turn, emphasizing a different word each time the sentence is read. Depending upon the tone and way the sentence is spoken, the same word conveys different meanings to different people. This exercise can provide a springboard into a discussion of barriers

---

[3]Holder, Kenneth P. "Introducing Students to Writing—and to Each Other." *Business Education Forum* 39:21-22; December 1984.

[4]Burtness, Paul S., and Hulbert, Jack E. *Effective Business Communication.* Eighth edition. Cincinnati: South-Western Publishing Co., 1985. p. 13.

to communication. Case studies, role-playing, and other activities give students practice in oral skills and experience in handling human relations at work.

Some business educators have students develop and make oral presentations. One method allows students to present short impromptu speeches to small groups. According to Dauwalder, these speeches can be ungraded learning exercises on familiar topics.[5] The organization of the short speech is similar to the organization of every communication: the main topic should be identified, the subtopics should be chosen to relate to the main idea, and then the overall organization of the speech should be chosen to reach a certain audience. Depending upon the purpose of the speech—to persuade, inform, or entertain—the organizational style will differ. Finally, students can critique each other's oral presentations. Any criticism given should be constructive since many students feel vulnerable and need positive reinforcement in developing and improving speaking skills.

READING. Because business students and employees need to understand written communications quickly, some business educators include separate reading units: discovering the main topic of the message, analyzing who is the intended reader, discussing the tone of the message, and evaluating the effectiveness of the message.

Daily class exercises can provide beneficial reading practice for students. For example, as students read a letter-writing exercise, they analyze and point out the purpose for the communication. Once students identify the reason for the communication and the main ideas to be conveyed, they determine what type of document to write.

Business educators can also develop their students' reading skills by assigning current articles. Students read the articles and then identify the main and supporting ideas. Article readings from current journals provide a wide assortment of topics—interpersonal skills, customer relations, changing organizational patterns, and others. Students can critique the articles by identifying the meaning, the tone, and the writer's point of view. By discussing potential audiences, students discover how each article is written to reach its intended audience. Still other business educators introduce readability formulas so that students understand the importance of writing at a reading level that is appropriate for the intended audience.

WRITING. Pretests and other diagnostic tools can help teachers of communication specialty courses identify weaknesses in students' English backgrounds. Individualized and group exercises provide remedial work that helps improve the English usage in students' writing. Even during language usage reviews, business educators can give students opportunities for reinforcement of their writing skills. Students can practice appositional or parenthetical commas in drills, for example, and then write their own sentences using these same constructions. Reading these sentences aloud or checking each other's sentences silently allows students to analyze the writing style of others and to focus on technical communication skills. Some students

[5]Dauwalder, David P. " 'Micro' Oral Presentation Applies Report-Writing Principles and Techniques." *Business Education Forum* 40:18-19; April 1986.

may need remedial work in identifying complete sentences before they can benefit fully from document-writing activities. Of course, the business English/communication courses allow for ample variety in types of writing activities—letters, memos, reports, and resumes.

Proofreading drills allow students to locate and correct errors by editing written work. Students can aid each other in refining their writing by checking each other's written work carefully. Using a cooperative approach to proofreading not only results in better quality written work but also provides an opportunity for interdependence and cooperation—both interpersonal communication skills needed on the job.

INCORPORATING ELECTRONIC MEDIA. Communication methods are changing with advances in electronic media. Field trips to local businesses can acquaint students with the current technologies available to facilitate communication. Business educators will want to schedule field trips to businesses for demonstrations of new technologies and for the continuing feedback from business people about the need for all business workers to have good communication skills.

For example, on a recent trip to one of Michigan's largest law firms, students learned that many communications involve computer terminals. If a message is taken for someone, it is placed in the person's message center on the computer; if a report needs to be sent to someone working in another department located on another floor, electronic mail within the company is used; if the message is to be sent to another division in this state or another state, a second form of electronic mail is used. Even lawyers keyboard their own documents into terminals; administrative assistants then make necessary revisions in grammar, spelling, and punctuation. Appointments, meetings, and conferences are scheduled through the computer. Paper and telephone-tag communications of the past are eliminated since the easy-to-use computer system allows the frequent informal communications to be stored and retrieved when convenient. Of course, good communication skills are still needed to create those messages.

There are many instructional strategies that secondary school business educators can use to help their students develop the communication skills that are needed in today's information society. Dynamic business educators will take advantage of the many opportunities to improve the listening, speaking, reading, and writing skills of students and to show them how electronic media facilitate communication.

Evaluation strategies. Evaluating basic communication skills need not be a formal procedure unless business educators choose to make it so. After completing a unit in listening skills, for example, business educators can check these skills daily when giving directions. The true test comes when students listen to instructions daily, respond in a way that shows understanding, and even repeat the directions to others. If the need for more formal evaluation becomes apparent, business educators can develop instructional units that would evaluate students' abilities to listen actively, to identify the main topic and supporting topics, and then to identify the details supporting the topics.

With the introduction of different circumstances into the business English/

communication course, teachers can evaluate students' abilities to comprehend the situation, organize the message around the main ideas, present relevant details, and provide an effective closing. The method chosen to present the communication will vary, but the organization of the message depends upon the audience, purpose of the message, desired tone, and main ideas. If a particular student is having difficulty in understanding the communication situation, the student's reading level should be checked. The student may be reading at a level well below the reading level of the instructional materials being used. Then the teacher can make remedial assignments, provide tutorial sessions, or refer the student to a reading specialist, if available, within the secondary school.

To formally evaluate letter, report, and speech assignments, business educators can use checklists from the teachers manuals that accompany most textbooks. Suggested general items for evaluation include the content, organization, language usage, and format of the message.

The possible topics for inclusion in the business English/communication course are vast, and business educators may need to be selective depending upon the available time, the needs of the students in the community, and the deficiencies identified in the school population. Whatever business English/communication course business educators choose to offer, listening, speaking, reading, and writing skills can be incorporated in daily lessons and reinforced throughout the course. Students can develop written and oral communication skills that will be useful to them throughout their lives. Since the course provides students with the language arts competencies that employers and society are demanding, English credit toward graduation should be given. A one-semester course will not provide all the answers to improved communication skills, but it will definitely help; additionally, all business educators must also integrate communication skills throughout the business curriculum.

INTEGRATING COMMUNICATION SKILLS
THROUGHOUT THE BUSINESS CURRICULUM

The business curriculum at the comprehensive high school provides education for and about business. It includes vocational courses for students who plan to get jobs directly out of high school and for students who plan to continue their educations before entering professions. It includes basic business education or general education courses for all students. The business curriculum should provide opportunities for all students to develop information skills; personal development skills; economic, consumer, and business concept skills; and technological skills. All basic communication skills—listening, speaking, reading, and writing—should also be integrated throughout the business curriculum. The scope of the business curriculum allows variety in the ways communication skills are developed. When all business educators in every business course stress the communication skills of listening, speaking, reading, and writing in an organized manner, the overall performance of business students can be improved tremendously.

Vocational and basic business educators must integrate communication skills throughout their offerings. Each course presents unique opportunities to build and reinforce different communication skills. The content in vocational business classes involves developing job-related skills, people-related skills, and employment-related skills. The course content in basic business education classes involves developing economics-related skills, business-related skills, and keyboard- and computer-related skills. These courses set the foundation for personal use and business applications and also provide unique opportunities for reinforcing basic communication skills.

Vocational offerings. The federal government funds vocational business programs in two major areas: business and office, and marketing and distribution. According to Malitz, business and office instructional programs prepare individuals to plan, organize, direct, and control all business office systems and procedures, while marketing and distribution instructional programs prepare individuals for occupations involving industrial and customer goods and services.[6]

BUSINESS AND OFFICE PROGRAMS. In business and office programs students acquire and perform many communication skills crucial to success in positions centered around the handling of information. Instruction includes creating, editing, printing, and storing of written communications and records. Good basic English skills are needed for success in document-preparation activities. While proofreading is a major part of all document-preparation activities, the process itself is usually taught step by step. First, students check punctuation, grammar, and spelling. Second, students check content and accuracy of information. Third, students check format details. Finally, students evaluate the document overall for effectiveness in achieving its purpose.

The review of English essentials can coincide with proofreading units. For example, students intensively review comma usage and then proofread exercises with built-in comma errors. This procedure continues until students can proofread any copy accurately. As students develop skill in editing, they begin transcription units. Students can use transcription equipment to produce documents that need the same punctuation, spelling, and grammar applications that they have studied in the English essentials unit and have reviewed in the proofreading exercises. This additional reinforcement allows students to transfer drill learning into practical applications. Applying these same proofreading techniques to all skill areas gives students confidence in their work and an ability to use technical communication skills appropriately.

During the development of shorthand skills, students also learn to punctuate, spell, and use correct grammar as part of their daily transcription assignments. Shorthand skill is still a prerequisite for many jobs that require good communication skills because employers know that people with good shorthand skills also have good language usage skills. As noted previously, the Wisconsin Department of Public Instruction issues one English credit for

---

[6]Malitz, Gerald S. *A Classification of Instructional Programs.* National Center for Education Statistics. Washington, D.C.: The Center, 1981.

110

a semester shorthand course because of the basic English skills inherent in the course content.

Skills in interpersonal relations and telephone techniques are developed using case studies and role-playing situations in business and office programs. Interpersonal communications among employees, clients and customers, and employers are the focus in face-to-face and telephone situations. Students learn to greet others courteously, determine the purpose of the interaction, and show interest in others while giving clear directions and pertinent information that follows company policies.

In planning telephone communications, students learn to gather all information pertaining to a call before placing the call. Similarly, many business people actually plan their telephone calls on paper before placing them. Keeping the purpose of the call clearly in mind, students plan and practice placing calls, identifying themselves, giving the purpose of the call, listening and showing understanding of what the receiver of the call is saying, and finally completing the call. Using a multiline teletrainer, students answer simulated company telephones correctly, determine the purpose of a call, transfer or respond to the call properly, and verify any information given or received. Students tactfully request information and interact with difficult callers while still projecting a positive company image through their telephone voices. Information received is verified to assure complete understanding between the caller and the person being called. Students then close the call on a positive note. Throughout the telephone unit students develop an ability to project a pleasing and helpful telephone personality that enhances the company image.

With the secretarial career ladder changing to include administrative assistant assignments, students may need to learn other communication skills. The administrative assistant sometimes uses telemarketing skills, which include planning and placing telephone calls to potential clients and getting clients to respond with the desired action. Knowledge of sales psychology and interpersonal skills are necessary for students to be able to control the conversation in order to direct action toward the desired outcome. These telemarketing communication skills are typically part of the marketing and distribution program.

Students can compare and contrast telephone and face-to-face communication. The tone of voice and manner of speaking are important elements of a telephone communication. In a face-to-face communication, body language and facial expressions are parts of the message. Students can develop an awareness of how their body language conveys messages to others, whether in job interviews or in situations with co-workers, superiors, or clients. As a separate unit or as a continuation of face-to-face communication, understanding of body language is essential for office employees. Business educators need to offer their students the experiences of understanding body language and of presenting positive images.

Business people are willing to work with students during job application and interview units to create a realistic atmosphere that will help students develop the best possible interview images of themselves. Frequently students hesitate during the interviewing process, and mock interviews that have been practiced, videotaped, or role-played build student confidence. Starting with newspaper want ads, students find what is realistically available in the job market that will match the skills they now possess. If word processing equipment is available, students can create resumes to match each interview situation. The application and thank-you or follow-up letters allow students to demonstrate their ability to communicate in written form with potential employers. If students telephone for actual appointments for the mock interviews, participating business people have an opportunity to assess and critique students' abilities to respond in telephone situations. The interview itself allows students to demonstrate spoken communication skills and then receive constructive feedback from business people before applying for real jobs. Business people often will travel to the classroom for these activities if time or distance does not allow students to go to them at their respective businesses.

MARKETING AND DISTRIBUTION PROGRAMS. Marketing and distribution instructional programs provide courses in analyzing the marketplace, examining promotional techniques, investigating pricing and distribution, and performing distribution activities. Students learn how the communication process is related to the promotion of goods and services. They apply human relation skills in selling activities. Good communication skills in listening, speaking, reading, and writing are vital to students who plan careers in marketing and distribution.

The customer's point of view needs to be understood by marketing and distribution students since customers are the most important part of any business. Marketing students study customers and their needs for goods or services. Then they learn how to provide the goods and services that satisfy those needs. Role-playing, case problems, and one-on-one or small-group exercises can demonstrate to students the power of personal communication skills in satisfying customers' needs.

Personal development skills typically learned by marketing students include positive personality traits, appropriate dress, and understanding of body language and personal space. Nonverbal cues, which are shown in the face, are also studied. Observing a customer's nonverbal cues is just as important to the outcome of a sale as what the customer actually says. The abilities to listen and to observe will alert students to appropriate sales tactics to follow in dealing with individual customers. Using each other as potential customers, students can practice these sales tactics and demonstrate good speech habits— speaking clearly and precisely, avoiding slang, giving complete and accurate information, and the like.

Marketing educators clearly can provide opportunities for business students to improve basic communication skills throughout marketing and distribution programs. As students become more aware of customers and how to influence them, students will understand the need to develop strong personal and professional communication skills.

Business educators have many opportunities in vocational courses to build effective communication skills. The ability to communicate with others is very important for students' success in personal and professional situations. Consequently, students need to develop written and oral communication skills throughout their vocational business programs.

Basic business education offerings. The basic business curriculum provides knowledge about economic education; business, marketing, and accounting functions; and keyboarding and computer literacy skills. Students may be exposed to these topics early in their school careers. In the elementary grades students have opportunities to explore the business world, examine careers, develop job attitudes and human relation skills, understand basic economic concepts, and learn keyboarding skills. During these activities students could interview business people and then report their findings in written or oral form. After learning to keyboard, students may compose simple letters or reports. Of course, elementary teachers already infuse basic communication skills through career awareness and basic economics activities.

Middle school teachers expand on these skills while building business concepts and refining keyboarding skills. Composing at the keyboard would allow students to develop ideas using complete sentences and still increase their keyboarding proficiency. Students could use a different work-related character trait each day as a warm-up composition exercise. For example, explaining what the trait of adaptability means by relating it to the world of work allows students to express themselves in complete sentences on impromptu topics and to develop appropriate work-related attitudes.

In basic economics courses middle school teachers develop lessons about business. Whether reading about and then discussing advantages and disadvantages associated with small businesses or exploring entrepreneurship, students can respond in writing or by speaking to questions about business organization. These exercises can be informally corrected during presentation or formally corrected using specific writing or speaking criteria.

At the high school level basic business education gives students the necessary understanding to fulfill their individual needs in the marketplace. The American economic system becomes realistic during simulated activities where self-management, interpersonal relations, critical thinking, and decision-making skills are part of the basic business curriculum. Throughout basic business courses, students examine business concepts and then make decisions about their applications. The Applied Economics course sponsored by Junior Achievement, for example, provides hands-on experience using a computer to simulate business enterprises.[7] In this course students make decisions about product development, marketing, and advertising that affect the profits and losses of businesses. These decisions also reinforce market and price concepts and the laws of supply and demand. Business representatives interact weekly with students, providing community resources and financial, economic, and technical knowledge. Business educators can reinforce basic communication skills daily as students make and justify business decisions, explore domestic and international markets, and interact

---

[7]Junior Achievement Incorporated. *Applied Economics—A Program of Junior Achievement.* Stamford, Conn.: Junior Achievement, 1985.

orally with representatives from the business community concerning the American enterprise system.

Business educators also strengthen the communication skills of students in basic business education courses. Business educators should use activities in every basic business course to develop students' listening, speaking, reading, and writing skills.

Business educators have many opportunities for integrating communication skills throughout the business curriculum. They can develop a wide variety of communication skills in classes that are parts of business and office and marketing and distribution programs. In addition, business educators can develop communication skills in classes that provide basic business education. As business educators integrate communication skills instruction in classes for and about business, they will strengthen the communication abilities of their students.

CONCLUSION

Elementary and middle school educators provide the communication foundation upon which high school business educators build vocational and basic business education. In each of the business course offerings at the secondary level, business educators have unique opportunities to develop and refine the basic communication skills of their students. The business English/communication specialty course provides an intensive review of the technical English skills and basic communication skills and applies them in business situations. Vocational and basic business education courses provide unique opportunities for building many different communication skills. When every business educator shares in the responsibility for developing the listening, speaking, reading, and writing skills of students, then business programs at the secondary level can truly be credited for providing lifelong skills. Business students will have the knowledge and skills to communicate effectively in their personal and professional lives and to compete successfully in the business world.

CHAPTER 12

Teaching Communication for Business
At the Postsecondary Level

LOIS J. BACHMAN

Community College of Philadelphia, Philadelphia, Pennsylvania

Business communication in the two-year college is usually a dichotomy, one-half business English and one-half business communication. Depending upon the number of courses in the entire business communication sequence, the two components may be offered together or separately. Colleges having only one course might have a combined business English and communication offering. But colleges with two or more courses in the sequence frequently have a freshman-level business English course and a sophomore-level comprehensive communication course.

In order to take a careful look at both business English and business communication offerings, a separate discussion of each course follows. The questions answered are: (1) Who takes the courses? (2) Who teaches the courses? (3) What is the suggested course content? (4) What are some effective methods of teaching the subjects? (5) What assignments are apropos, and what are their purposes? (6) What evaluation systems are recommended? (7) What are the major concerns of professors and students in the business communication sequence? Business English will be examined first because it usually precedes a comprehensive business communication course.

BUSINESS ENGLISH

Students who take the course. A separate course entitled Business English (or Business Communications I) is frequently included in a one-year office certificate program and in two-year office administration, secretarial science, office science, and word processing associate degree curriculums. It is usually a 100-level college course preceding a more advanced letter writing and report writing business communication course. Enrollment also includes students in two-year business education transfer programs for teacher training and one-year general business certificate students. The latter, who major in accounting, retailing, management, and other business areas, frequently take business English in lieu of English composition. In addition to the students who are required to register for business English, there are some students who enroll in the course just to reinforce their basic English skills.

Faculty who teach the course. In some institutions, business English classes are taught by faculty members in the English department. Since full-time faculty frequently prefer English literature and essay courses to business English sections, the latter are often relegated to part-time English faculty.

The situation may be quite different in colleges that permit business education professors to teach business English classes. Usually the business English course, which stresses vocabulary, usage, style, and mechanics, tends to be a very popular choice among full-time business education faculty. Part-time business faculty assignments do evolve, however, when (1) there are too many sections to be staffed by full-timers, (2) the sections are offered at unpopular times, or (3) the sections are located at off-campus sites.

Appropriate content. Business English professors tend to rely on the assigned textbook to guide the contents of their course. Typical course coverage may include an introduction to business English; dictionary usage; spelling; words frequently misused (synonyms and homonyms); parts of speech; subjects and predicates; sentence patterns, phrases, and clauses; punctuation usage; capitalization; using numbers in business English; writing effective sentences (avoiding fragments, run-on sentences); business English applications; and business vocabulary. The precise order of the topics to be included will vary depending upon the professor's preference and textbook table of contents.

Effective methods of teaching. Depending upon the professor's enthusiasm and motivation, a course of this type can range from dull, repetitive, routine, and boring to fast-moving and challenging. The subject matter needs an innovative approach to prevent rote memorization of principles, a brief application of the memorized rules, and a lack of carry-over to authentic business writing. To challenge their students and help them to master the material, a majority of successful business English professors use their own creations, in addition to textbook exercises and software. Here are some noteworthy techniques being used today in the postsecondary colleges:

1. The professor previews the chapter in class before asking the students to read the principles, do any programmed self-checks, or complete the end-of-chapter exercises. Pointing out the main components of the chapter plus any mnemonic devices or unusual learning helps can pave the way to student understanding and enthusiasm.

2. Frequent use of overhead projectors and transparencies allow those in attendance to focus on one section of an application exercise at a time. This excellent teaching device is usually welcomed by the students.

3. Students complete brief programmed self-checks at frequent intervals, without teacher feedback, to check their competency level and determine if they are meeting their short-term goals. This encourages students who have not mastered the material to reread prior chapters until they achieve an acceptable skill level.

4. Exercises reinforcing proper use of synonyms, homonyms, and business vocabulary can be assigned to teams of students. Team members work together in or out of class to complete the exercises and write effective sentences and short paragraphs using correct vocabulary. Ultimately, each team submits one paper reflecting the work of all its members.

5. Fast-paced spelling, subject-verb agreement, and vocabulary "bees" can

be scattered intermittently throughout the course, with a nonmonetary prize awarded to the winning half of the class.

6. Colorful, creative posters and flip chart pages that are appropriate for first- and second-level college students covering subject-verb agreement, homonym usage, punctuation benefits, and overall mechanical precision can accompany other teaching techniques and enliven the subject matter.

7. Clever, apropos cartoons gleaned from newspapers and magazines join other creative artwork distributed by the professor to add some humor to the course content.

8. Periodically, fun exercises can be completed in class. Two such examples are (1) lists of well-known cliches that are disguised when written in a very high level of diction and (2) sentences that have different meanings depending upon the placement of internal punctuation.

9. Recently journal, magazine, and newspaper articles that discuss the virtues of mechanical precision in a business setting and the use of preferred business vocabulary are distributed to the class. After students read them, lively discussion can ensue.

10. Using up-to-date computer-assisted software for teaching and reinforcement is particularly popular now that many more colleges are equipped with personal computers for computer-aided instruction. There are a number of software programs available to junior college professors should they be interested in using them. As can be expected, however, the programs have some flaws intermingled with their inherent strengths. Although it is difficult to find a single resource that lists business English software for college students, searching through microcomputer software catalogues, computer magazines, and vendor sales promotion literature will lead to the names and descriptions of apropos software. Also, personnel in college libraries and teaching centers may serve as excellent resource people.

It is worthwhile to note that many of the programs written for twelfth-grade high school students appear to meet the needs of the freshman-sophomore level business English student. In addition to external vendors, most publishers are now publishing textbooks with accompanying computer software programs. Therefore, the business English professor may wish to consult with a publisher's sales representative to locate software paralleling a selected text. In fact, it may not be too long before a textbook without accompanying software will not be considered for adoption.

A few questions to consider when selecting computer software are: (1) Can it be used on your equipment? (2) Does it meet your students' needs? (3) How easy is it to use? (4) How accessible is it for your students? (5) What is its cost?

Suggested assignments. In order to master the correct application of business English principles, it is necessary for the students to do a variety of exercises. The assignments, completed in class or at home, should be checked by the professor, and evaluative feedback should be given to the class. A variation in procedure will prevent filling in exercise forms from becoming a perfunctory activity. Alternating between individual and team assignments is one of many interesting assignment techniques.

Business English courses, because of their diversified content, suggest a variety of exercises. The following is a list of exercise topics that are appropriate for classroom or homework assignments:

1. Reviewing usage of homonyms
2. Precision in word usage
3. Spelling pretest and speed-spell exercises
4. Vocabulary skill exercises asking for definitions and usage in sentences
5. Punctuation exercises
6. Capitalization exercises and exercises using numbers
7. Sentence fragments, run-on sentences, and comma-splice errors
8. Dictionary skill exercises that include asking for word definitions, correct spelling, parts of speech, word division, and synonyms
9. Parts of speech exercises requesting plural and possessive forms, pronoun antecedents, comparison of adjectives and adverbs, correct form of verbs and pronouns, identification of parts of speech, and the selection of correct prepositions and conjunctions
10. Identifying subjects, verbs, direct and indirect objects, objective complements, objects of prepositions, predicate nominatives and adjectives, and appositives
11. Identifying prepositional, gerund, participial, and infinitive phrases
12. Dependent and independent clause exercises identifying noun, adjective, and adverbial clauses
13. Exercises correcting dangling verbals and nonparallel structure
14. Sentence revision exercises and composition of a variety of sentences
15. Composition of short easy-to-write communications applying business English principles
16. Proofreading exercises requiring students to first encircle errors in punctuation, grammar, spelling, parts of speech, capitalization, subject-verb agreement, and use of numbers and then produce a revised corrected copy.

Methods of evaluation. Evaluative procedures vary from one institution to another because of college policies, departmental practices, or professors' preferences. Any variations of the following might be satisfactory:

Component	*Percentage*
Homework and class participation	10%
Scores on tests given throughout the semester (5-8 tests)	60%
Spelling and vocabulary quizzes given frequently	10%
Final examination	20%
	100%

Professors may wish to drop the lowest test grade if departmental policy supports this policy.

Grading scales frequently follow either of these two variations:

A = 90-100	OR	A = 90-100
B = 80-89		B = 80-89
C = 75-79		C = 70-79

D = 70-74   D = 60-69
F = below 70   F = below 60

In addition, there is the bell curve used by many business English professors, assuring an even grade distribution.

Students who earn less than a B grade for the course usually exhibit weak writing skills in the more advanced letter and report writing course.

Concerns about the course. Professors and students of business English express a number of concerns, some more vehemently than others. Primary among their concerns are (1) the lack of skill carry-over to related courses, (2) the lack of subject retention, (3) the lack of importance placed on the subject matter, and (4) the difficulty experienced receiving college transfer credit for business English. A short discussion of each one of these problems follows.

LACK OF SKILL CARRY-OVER. Students have been known to receive A or B grades in business English but fail to use correct subject-verb agreement, pronouns, and verb forms in English composition, business communication, office procedures, and transcription courses. From a student's standpoint, what is taught in one classroom doesn't appear to apply to the course content in other classrooms. There is frequently insufficient carry-over. This lack of continuity is very frustrating for the business educator.

LACK OF SUBJECT RETENTION. Studies that apply to the teaching of business English courses in isolation have produced fairly consistent results. The statistics appear to indicate that writing and proofreading exercises that require students to apply the principles help them retain what they have learned in business English. Conversely, memorizing many rules with little opportunity to apply them in writing assignments leads to lack of retention.

LACK OF IMPORTANCE. A de-emphasis on the need for acquiring spelling and grammar skills has arisen recently because of the increased capabilities of computer software. The belief that computer keyboarders can rely on computer capabilities to correct composition skills is downgrading the value of business English courses. Until students, professors, and administrators realize the full value of mastering the principles of business English, it may be an uphill battle in the classroom.

LACK OF CREDIT TRANSFERABILITY. Many students in the secretarial science and office science curriculums are unconcerned about the difficulty in transferring business English credit, for they earn their associate degrees to obtain full-time employment. Their immediate career goals do not include transferring to a baccalaureate degree institution. On the other hand, general business students, many of whom would profit from a business English elective, are dissuaded from enrolling in the course because of the nontransferability to many business administration degree programs. Although the American Assembly of Collegiate Schools of Business (AACSB) has recently recognized the value of business communication, the same recognition does not extend to business English courses.

Each one of these concerns is a deterrent to achieving the objectives of business educators who value the mastery of business English for all business students. Unfortunately, in many two-year colleges, the objective of students' reaching and maintaining competency levels in business English appears to be an elusive dream.

BUSINESS COMMUNICATION

Students who take the course. In some two-year colleges, the diversity of enrollees follows the same pattern as that in business English. There are more students majoring in office science, secretarial science, word processing, and office administration than in other curriculums. A recent trend indicates, however, that business communication is being added to some business administration and general business curriculums, requiring its completion by all business majors. This may be partly attributable to the recent enthusiastic acceptance of business communication by AACSB.

Faculty who teach the course. Because of the diverse nature of business communication, faculty assigned to teach the course usually find that it is a very challenging assignment. Depending upon the college's policy, business communication is taught by business or English faculty. Those in the business faculty that appear to be the most prepared to teach business communication are business educators, who also provide instruction in business English and transcription.

In order to offer a dynamic, meaningful course, the English faculty teaching business communication must acquire firm knowledge of current business practice. Expertise in the teaching of written and oral communication without business acumen shortchanges the avid business communication student.

Appropriate content. Professors of business communication who have been teaching the course many years have accumulated many magazine articles, business letters and memos, and assorted helpful hints to supplement the contents of the required textbook. Thus, the contents of the course will be guided by the depth of the professor's teaching file plus the textbook coverage of the subject. The answers to the following questions will help to determine the course content:

1. How many class hours are available to cover the material?
2. Do you wish to offer a comprehensive business communication course?
3. Is it your intention to stress letter writing over report writing?
4. Do you plan to include oral communication topics, such as listening, telephone usage, public speaking, nonverbal communication, dictating, and interviewing?
5. How much time will you devote to communication theory, writing styles, and format and mechanics?

The list that follows mentions a wide range of topics that may be included in a one-semester business communication course in a two-year college:

- Introduction to business communication
- Communication theory
- Barriers to effective communication
- Mechanical, factual, and verbal precision
- Preferred writing styles

- Proper tone and the *you-concept*
- Letter and memo writing—routine messages, good news, goodwill, complaints, collection letters, adjustment, bad news, persuasive letters
- Report writing—short and long reports
- Proposal writing
- Agenda and minutes of meetings
- Employment communications
- Oral communications—listening, telephone use, public speaking skills, nonverbal communication, dictating, interviewing
- Communication in the electronic office.

Since time rarely permits coverage of all the topics, the business communication professor will first determine the general and specific objectives of the course and then include those topics that will help achieve the objectives.

Effective methods of teaching. Unlike business English, which can be routine and repetitive, business communication is usually quite interesting and fast-moving, even invigorating and challenging for the class. Students have many past experiences to share with their classmates, experiences in both work and social communications. This input, together with the professor's up-to-date knowledge of the subject, lends itself well to diversified methods of teaching. Some less obvious techniques could include the use of:

1. Team projects in which each team member must carry his/her weight in finishing the assignments
2. Peer evaluation of students' written assignments
3. Interview role-plays using students, professors, and college job placement specialists as the actors
4. Computer-assisted instruction to compose, edit, and revise letters and memos
5. Overhead projectors to critique textbook and student communications
6. Current videotapes and films that are discussed after they are shown
7. Humorous and challenging handouts from the professor's files to inform and amuse the class, including such things as cartoons, exercises, communications, and short articles
8. Business, government, and college employees who have business communication responsibilities serving as guest lecturers and allowing themselves to be queried by the class
9. Videotaping students who are making oral presentations. The individuals view the videotapes privately to critique themselves and discuss their findings with their professors.

The methods of teaching must be varied and unpredictable to keep the students on their toes and keep them interested. There is no doubt that monotonous lecturing and daily reading of the textbook aloud has no place in a business communication class.

Suggested assignments. The diversity of a comprehensive business communication course lends itself well to a variety of assignments that are both stimulating and educational. Professors who subscribe to the theory that in order to write well, one must practice writing will certainly give many writing assignments. Some assignments will require students to write sentences; others will result in letters or memos or short reports. Regardless of the format assigned, all student submissions should be critiqued by the professor and returned to the writer. This evaluative procedure requires many hours of critical reading on the part of the professor. A teacher who is unwilling to spend time out of class evaluating students' written projects should refuse to accept a business communication teaching assignment.

Some assignments will originate from end-of-chapter exercises and case studies in the required textbook or its accompanying student activity edition. Others will come from the professor's personal file of "My Favorite Assignments." Others may be suggested by colleagues at professional conferences or in professional journals. The source of assignments is relatively unimportant. What is important are the following factors:

1. All assignments should pertain to the material discussed in class.
2. They should offer a distinct opportunity for growth for the students.
3. Their undertaking should provide a challenging experience and their fulfillment a sense of satisfaction.
4. The time they take for completion should be reasonable in light of the students' total work load.
5. Some assignments should have the right ingredients to serve as vehicles for team undertakings. This will stimulate both cooperative and competitive feelings.

Methods of evaluation. Professors who are wary of assigning grades for daily or weekly out-of-class assignments contend that letter grades encourage cheating. Students who have weak written communication skills may solicit help from student achievers and relatives to camouflage their own lack of competency. To discourage cheating, some professors suggest giving credit (ν) and no credit (N/C) evaluations. This enables all students to eventually convert the N/C's to ν's after correction, revision, and timely resubmission. The professor guides the resubmission all the way. At the end of the term, the total number of ν's earned will establish a student's assignment grade.

Naturally, the weighting of the different components of a comprehensive business communication course will vary; what works well for one professor may not work for another. Whatever weighting system is selected, it is important to keep in mind that objective critiquing is required and the use of evaluation checklists with a point distribution is recommended. This will eliminate subjective evaluation when determining grades for tests and major projects and the giving of credit for the shorter assignments.

A brief look at one acceptable evaluation procedure follows:

Component	Percentage
Class/home assignments (ν's)	30%
Midterm examination	20%
Short report	20%
Employment communication project	10%

Final examination	<u>20%</u>
	100%

Concerns about the course. Two primary concerns expressed in the discussion of business communication are the lack of skill carry-over and the lack of universal communication requirements.

LACK OF SKILL CARRY-OVER. The lack of skill carry-over is a common concern about business English and business communication. The competencies acquired in a comprehensive business communication course should equip students to handle most communication assignments in management, marketing, and office procedures courses. Unfortunately, this does not seem to be the situation. Why students do not carry over their skills to related courses is a mystery to many business educators, a mystery that needs to be solved if a student's overall education is to be cumulative and effective.

LACK OF UNIVERSAL COMMUNICATION REQUIREMENTS. The lack of universal communication requirements also creates concerns, especially in the two-year colleges that require the business communication sequence in only office administration curriculums and one-year certificate programs in business. Down the line, this can lead to support staff, such as administrative assistants and word processing secretaries, knowing more about letter and report writing than many of the managers. The shortsightedness of curriculum committees who undervalue business communication courses for all business majors contributes to the number of poorly written communications generated by many decision makers in industry.

CONCLUSION

The teaching of business English in a two-year college has not changed appreciably in the last 20 years. Although many new textbooks have appeared on the market, giving the professors many options, the material in the texts is fairly similar. True, the lists of business vocabulary are periodically updated and the proofreading exercises reflect today's business jargon, but the subject has not essentially changed. It is only the accompaniment of software packages that has given the course a new look and a much needed lift.

Similarly, the letter and report writing communication course has significantly improved with the acquisition of personal computers. The influx of word processing software has made a considerable impact on the teaching methods presently in vogue. With grant money providing the funding to purchase hardware, computer-assisted instruction in the teaching of business communication is becoming quite popular. In fact, many professors who are not using computers in their courses are beginning to feel inadequate in front of those who do. By the mid 1990's the use of computers will be every bit as commonplace as the use of chalkboards and overhead projectors.

The expanded coverage of business communication in the electronic office and the impact of computers in the classroom have enhanced teaching effectiveness. Business educators are aware of this. They also know, however, that although business communication proficiency is needed by all business students, many curriculum committees and administrators have disregarded this need. Perhaps it is the difficulty in transferring credits that has influenced the decision not to include the courses in business curriculums. Or perhaps they are not fully acquainted with the contents and value of these courses. Whatever the reason may be, it is up to business educators in two-year colleges to assume some responsibility.

Until the majority of business students acquire strong skills in business communication, business educators should campaign for the inclusion of a business communication sequence in all postsecondary business curriculums.

CHAPTER 13

Teaching Communication for Business
At the Undergraduate Level

DONALD J. LEONARD
Arizona State University, Tempe

For a number of diverse reasons, no facet of undergraduate business education has been subject to more change in recent decades than has the business communication component. At some four-year undergraduate schools, the communication requirement has been eliminated from the core; and in some cases, the basic communication course has been phased out of existence or given to some other college. At other schools, the communication discipline has thrived and blossomed from one basic course offering to numerous offerings at various levels—enough, in some instances, to comprise a major area of study.

Though the forces and counterforces responsible for these drastically different destinies can be quite intriguing, their complexity renders them beyond the scope of this treatise. This chapter will instead describe, with primary focus on the basic course, the communication curriculum that might be developed for a four-year business college. It presupposes a climate wherein the significance of the communication discipline is recognized and appreciated.

BASIC BUSINESS COMMUNICATION

At regional and national conventions and at less formal gatherings of business communication teachers, three strategic conversational topics invariably arise. These topics all relate to the common bond among these teachers: the basic business communication class that they all teach or have taught at one time or another.

These topics are (1) the course's content at the different schools represented, (2) the various ways in which the course is being delivered to the students (along with related environmental factors), and (3) the manner in which the students are evaluated.

No one can deny that the basic business communication course at most universities has changed appreciably in the last two or three decades. These changes, however, have been variously depicted as an evolution or growth by some and as an erosion by others.

Without presenting judgments of one kind or another, this section will review these three subjects of course content, delivery systems, and student evaluations. These subjects will be treated in terms of historical precedence and options now available.

Course content. Twenty to 30 years ago, life was fairly clear and fixed for teachers of business communication. The course focus was clearly written communication in business. Some teachers may have given less attention than others to reports, but they all recognized that a full semester could easily be devoted to improving the business writing skills of their students. Some of these teachers attempted to give a degree of attention to oral communication, but even those teachers regretted that they had to take emphasis from the written word to give some to the spoken word.

During the 1970's, many business communication teachers became interested in the more encompassing field of organizational communication. Early in the decade, the Academy of Management created a separate division for members interested in the field of organizational communication. In the American Business Communication Association, this interest built to the point that the 1976 national convention in San Diego featured a panel discussion entitled, "The Present and Future of Organizational Communication in the Business Communication Course."

Instructors who chose to blend organizational communication topics into their business communication courses generally reported favorable results. They noted that their students were quite receptive and even enthusiastic about reviewing subjects such as conflict resolution, the grapevine, group communication, nonverbal communication, listening, and interviewing.

Such reports, however, were not universal and were not always well received by colleagues. Many business communication teachers believed quite strongly that there simply wasn't enough time in one semester to do justice to both business communication and organizational communication. They saw the inclusion of these other subject areas as an erosion of the quality of the business communication teaching/learning experience. The issue was never fully resolved; and in some circles, the debate still rages.

With the organizational communication controversy not yet fully put to rest, the 1980's injected new fuel into the fire of the course breadth/depth issue. By far the most pervasive and far-reaching development to burst upon the scene was that of technologically mediated communication. Technologies such as mirocomputers, electronic mail, teleconferencing, networking, and computer graphics have all worked to change dramatically the ways in which people communicate in business. Consequently, these technologies have similarly changed the nature of the business communication course taught at many universities and colleges.

Nonetheless, one can still find a contingent of dedicated traditional business communication teachers who note that regardless of the technology employed, a business communicator must still be versed in the principles of language conventions, letters, memos, and reports—written and oral. They can readily demonstrate that such subjects easily consume a full semester of attention.

One other subject area has found its way into the basic business communication class at many four-year colleges and universities. Since the American Assembly of Collegiate Schools of Business (AACSB) recommended that undergraduate business programs incorporate international business into their curriculums, most business schools have done so in one of three ways. Some have created new classes to present the various aspects of international business to their students. Some have worked the subject into existing courses. Finally, some have developed a combination of the two preceding approaches.

While the subject of intercultural communication could easily command a full semester's attention, a teacher could still give an adequate introduction to the subject in a much smaller course module. Such a module could focus upon the ever-shrinking world community or "global village" and the accelerating likelihood of the students' eventual involvement in some form of international business. Such a treatment could also review inherent barriers to intercultural communication and some guidelines for the world business traveler and expatriot.

Having reviewed some of the historical developments in the basic business communication course taught at four-year colleges and universities, this chapter will next present a sample course outline. Before this outline is presented, however, recognition should be given to the fact that course content is not always subject solely to the instructor's discretion. Numerous external factors play a part in ultimately determining what may or may not be taught in the basic business communication course.

Perhaps the most obvious of these external factors is the resource support provided the instructor(s). Without the necessary hardware and software, one cannot provide more than a passing glance at word processing and computer graphics technologies. Without access to a teleconferencing facility, one cannot vividly demonstrate the blessings and blemishes of this development.

The business college administration and faculty (where faculty governance exists) might also have a say in the business communication course content. Furthermore, in state schools, where credit transfer arrangements are made through articulation, another "representative" voice might need to be heard before any changes are made in the content of the basic business communication course. Finally, the course delivery system may well determine that certain subjects may or may not be treated.

The following sample course outline is the one now used in the teaching of the basic business communication course at Arizona State University. It is offered here only as a sample and certainly not as the last word in how such a course might be taught.

This particular course organization evolved from the influence of a number of the factors reviewed in the preceding paragraphs. The fact that the course gives considerable emphasis to oral and written reports and relatively little attention to letters is an outgrowth of a college ad hoc core committee's recommendation. That same committee also recommended that the new course be taught at the junior level. It is still, however, taught at the sophomore level because of the transfer credit issue previously referenced.

Finally, the content was partly influenced by the delivery system necessitated by limited resources and increasing enrollments. For these reasons, a megalecture/discussion class arrangement was first employed in the fall 1986 semester. Under this arrangement, the students attend one megalecture (in groups of 300) each week for 75 minutes and one 35-student discussion class each week, which also lasts 75 minutes. The general intent is that the lecture cover the theories, concepts, and guidelines while the discussion class focuses on the specific assignments. The following outline provides the topics covered during the megalecture each week.

Basic Business Communication Course Outline

Week	1	Course Introduction
Week	2	Oral Presentations (focus on briefings)
Week	3	Listening
Week	4	First Examination
Week	5	Writing Style and Tone
Week	6	Organization Plans for External Company Communication
Week	7	Career Planning and Communication
Week	8	Second Examination
Week	9	Report Planning and Data Collection
Week	10	Visual Aids
Week	11	Report Format
Week	12	Third Examination
Week	13	Interpersonal Communication in Business
Week	14	Organizational Communication
Week	15	Intercultural Communication
Week	16	Final Examination (cumulative)

Delivery systems. Having reviewed the many subject areas that might be treated in a basic business communication course, this chapter will now examine the various delivery systems available. Additionally, this section will recognize the contemporary controversy surrounding the process and product approaches to teaching business writing.

Just as the course content was relatively stable 20 to 30 years ago, so was the delivery system. Because the course focused on writing and because the grading of assignments took so many out-of-class hours, school administrators recognized that classes had to be kept small. If business communication teachers were to accomplish their proposed mission of improving their students' writing skills, they had to give ample feedback through numerous assignments. They could not do so with more than 25 to 30 students.

Graduate teaching assistants were sometimes used, but these aides were only as effective as the selection and training procedures applied to them. Furthermore, such graduate teaching assistants were usually available only at sizable institutions with, of course, graduate programs.

Some such schools, with adequate technical and human resources, experimented in the 1960's and 1970's with a televised presentation of at least part of the course. Louisiana State University (LSU) in Baton Rouge was one such school. The business communication lecture there was televised twice each week for 50 minutes to classes of 200 students. For the third period, the students met in groups of approximately 40 to discuss cases and assignments with teaching assistants.

Research done on the LSU television experience, compared to the small-class approach, concluded that the quality of the teaching/learning experience did not differ appreciably between the two delivery systems. The students learned as well and performed at about the same level in the two approaches. Attitudes of the students involved in the two approaches, however, did differ considerably. They much preferred the more personal setting of the smaller classroom.

With increasing enrollments and/or declining resources, coupled with a research thrust that seems to favor fewer classroom contact hours, many colleges and universities are now scrutinizing innovative or at least different delivery systems. The megalecture/discussion class approach is one such system that is more common today than it was ten years ago.

The megalecture may be delivered in person several times or televised. The discussion classes might be conducted by teaching assistants or full-time faculty. The number of students, furthermore, in attendance at the mega-lecture would be influenced by enrollments and facilities available. A mega-lecture to 300 to 500 students is not uncommon at schools committed to this approach.

The jury is still out with regard to a final verdict on this teaching approach in general—and in particular, as applied to business communication. Though many teachers claim that it is a workable solution to the problems facing them, just as many (if not more) business communication teachers protest adamantly that this approach prevents them from doing the job they should be doing and ultimately does a great disservice to the student. As in the case of the government's testing of new medications, more is likely to be known in years to come about possible side effects of this delivery system.

Before reviewing the process and product approaches to business writing, one other delivery strategy must be noted. Where resources and facilities permit, computer-assisted instruction can be used in conjunction with any of the delivery systems just described. Such instructional software is available with many of the latest business communication texts and revisions. Perhaps the major advantage of such software packages is that they can relieve the business communication instructor of the remedial work on language conventions that may have previously consumed an inordinate part of the basic business communication course.

One other delivery-related issue that has been receiving considerable attention lately is the process approach to teaching business writing. In fact, this topic was the subject of the entire winter 1987 issue of *The Journal of Business Communication*.

Proponents of this approach require their students to plan, draft, evaluate, revise, and edit. They claim that forcing the students to engage in these activities improves the quality of their writing. Proponents further claim that teachers who insist on teaching about the end product of the writing process are still in the dark ages.

Opponents counter that the process people have developed nothing new and that their descriptions of the process approach are often vague and in defiance of the writing principles that business communication teachers ought to be teaching. Opponents further contend that the writing process is unique to the writer; consequently, it would be wrong to try to force all writers into one process mold. Finally, the doubters point out that given all the subjects that teachers must now attempt to address in the basic course, time limitations would not permit the students to go through all the steps in the process approach for all assignments given in one semester.

Teachers and writers who are neither strongly for or against the process approach note that the process and product approaches need not be either/or choices. One can teach the process approach as one option that writers might try. Some would find it useful, and some would find it too regimented and time-consuming. At the same time, one can still examine and evaluate products to infer appropriate and successful processes.

Evaluations of students. Just as most managers face appraising subordinates' performances with absolute dread, many business communication teachers, especially new ones, claim that the grading of assignments is the very worst part of their jobs. For a number of reasons, the chore of sitting in judgment does not come naturally to most people. Add to that chore the very tedious nature of evaluating 100 to 150 versions of the same assignment, and one has a rather bleak picture of how a weekend or a week per assignment might have to be spent.

Bits and pieces of the tedium might be eliminated by software packages that check grammar and spelling. Furthermore, injecting an element of variety into each student's assignment might further reduce grading monotony. Teachers might accomplish the same grading monotony reduction by allowing the students a certain degree of freedom in choosing the exact nature of their assignments. Tedium considerations aside, however, some teachers believe that they can be more thorough in their grading when all students have done the same assignment.

Whether software packages are applied and whether the students complete the same or different assignments, the tedious nature of grading papers will never be completely annihilated. On the other hand, the judgment aspect of the grading process can be made less painful for the teacher and the student. This goal can be accomplished by applying to the grading process many of the same qualities that teachers insist upon seeing in their students' work.

Specificity is one such quality. Students want to know *why* they received a particular grade. They want to know what they did wrong and the severity of each wrongdoing. One way to send the latter message is to vary the actual size of the comments made on the paper. Another, and perhaps more common, way is to report separate grades for paper qualities such as content, organization and style.

These separate grades (along with supportive comments and a cumulative grade) are especially useful for shorter assignments such as letters and memos.

For longer assignments, such as intermediate or long reports, one might wish to divide the grading by report parts and apply the qualities of content, organization, and style to each part. For oral presentations, one might evaluate content, organization, style, and delivery with a form that includes specific descriptors of what these qualities entail.

Another student assignment quality that is easily recommended to graders, but not so easily attained, is positiveness. Assignments returned to students are usually filled with recommendations for improvements. The students generally view these recommendations as criticism, and thus as negative. It may take a truly outstanding feat to warrant a grader's praise on a student's paper.

Of course, one way to reduce the negative impact of returned papers would be to increase the commentary on good paper features. Some teachers, however, would regard this tactic as too time-consuming and would note that their primary charge is to show students how to improve their writing. They might further note that unmarked passages on a student's paper might be interpreted to mean that the passage is acceptable.

One other way of reducing the negative feedback on papers is the use of peer evaluations followed by the opportunity for a rewriting. A related technique is a teacher evaluation followed by a rewriting opportunity for an improved grade. The final grade on the assignment might be the higher of the two grades or an average of the two grades.

Related to the two preceding suggestions is one other way of lessening the blow of negative feedback. The teacher could return the earliest papers marked up, but with no grade assigned. In so doing, the teacher provides useful tips for potential performance improvement; and the student gets these tips at no cost or penalty.

Finally, on the point of the negative/positive reaction, some instructors believe that students "see red" when they get papers back because they literally see red—red ink. Such instructors think that the red ink symbolizes a moral wound inflicted upon the paper and the student's ego. To reduce the likelihood of this imagery, these teachers grade their papers with blue, black, or green ink—any color other than the dreaded red.

Whatever the tactic employed, be it one or more of the preceding techniques or a verbal explanation, students must be convinced that instructors are working on their behalf. This persuasive challenge must be met if they are to come to view the basic business communication course as a positive learning experience.

Credibility and increasing intensity are other qualities of the grading process that instructors should strive to attain. The students must believe that mistakes will reduce the quality and value of their work, and they must be motivated to take advantage of earlier feedback. Most teachers, however, with 100 to 150 students would be hard pressed to remember all the comments made on each student's earlier assignments. One way to work around the memory lapse and instill a sense of accountability in students is to have them hand in all previous assignments with each new one. A teacher can then warn students that repeated infractions will result in stiffer penalties. Most students will take the hint and start looking over previous assignments as they put together new ones.

Another message quality that instructors ought to incorporate into the grading process is timeliness. Although some students might have mixed emotions about getting feedback, most are eager to find out how they have done on assignments. So most teachers return papers to their classes as soon as they can.

Instructors also need to encourage timeliness in the submission of assignments. Late penalties—perhaps 5 or 10 percent of the value of the assignment per calendar day—can be a help in accomplishing this goal.

Missed exams provide a related dilemma. To discourage such misses, a teacher who gives objective or objective and subjective exams to the class might give totally essay makeup exams. With extremely large classes, however, makeup exams become, at best, a nightmare. One might avoid them altogether by giving enough exams to allow the student to drop the lowest grade or by adding the value of one missed exam to the value of the final exam.

One final point on evaluating students relates more to the nature of assignments than to their grading. Group writing projects are not uncommon in business, and so there is some precedence for their class use in longer report assignments. Furthermore, as class size increases appreciably at some schools, group writing projects carry the additional blessing of keeping one's grading load manageable. But some students strongly dislike group projects because not all students are willing to share the responsibility for assignment completion. One way to work around their apprehension is to incorporate a peer evaluation into the grading process. In so doing, however, a teacher must impress upon the students the need to evaluate productivity and not personality.

Whatever the grading procedures employed and whatever the class policies adopted by a teacher, probably the most important thing to remember is that these procedures and policies must be announced to the students *before* they are put into operation. Injustice—even perceived injustice—is quite possibly the worst enemy of teacher/student relations and ultimately of the teaching/learning process.

ORGANIZATIONAL/MANAGERIAL COMMUNICATION

A business communication course offering that has gained popularity at many four-year colleges and universities within the last 15 to 20 years is one called organizational communication or managerial communication. Whether called by the former or latter name, the courses are usually fairly similar in content and are typically aimed at helping administrators or future administrators to become better communicators within an organizational context.

Course content. Though the course content might be organized in a variety of ways, two fairly popular options will be described here. The first is generally inductive, and the second is more deductive.

The inductive approach goes from the specific to the general under the assumption that one must understand the parts of the whole before one can fully appreciate the complexity of that whole. This approach thus moves from the specific topic of intrapersonal communication to the next level of analysis, that of interpersonal communication, to the encompassing subject of organizational communication.

The first course section, intrapersonal communication, might also be labeled the psychology of human communication. Its goal would be to help students fully understand what happens when a human being attempts to engage in the process of communication. This goal might be facilitated by a look at some of the many models of communication available. An implicit goal of this section would be the provision of insight into the complexity of the entity with whom these future administrators will be attempting to interact through the communication process.

The second section of this inductive approach, interpersonal communication, builds upon the foundation established in the first section. Likely subjects for treatment here would be prerequisites for effective interpersonal communication, barriers to interpersonal communication, and guidelines for successful interpersonal communication. Interpersonal conflict resolution might also be studied here because of the pervasive nature of such conflict in modern organizations.

The final subsection of the inductive approach would be organizational communication. This course part could be organized according to structural aspects (upward/downward, formal/informal, meetings, interviews, etc.) and functional aspects (informative, instructive, directive, and persuasive).

The deductive approach begins with an introductory overview covering the communication process, managerial communication styles, organizational personalities, and formal/informal organizational communication systems. The second section would cover specific managerial communication skills of writing, speaking, listening, and nonverbal astuteness. The deductive approach would end with a coverage of the activities in which the preceding skills might be applied. Interviews, meetings, motivation, conflict resolution, negotiation, stress management, time management, and technologically mediated communication would all be subjects suitable for treatment in this last course subdivision.

Course delivery. Since this course is usually a junior- or senior-level class, and not required for most business majors, the small-class approach is the normal delivery method. Furthermore, due to the level and maturity of the students, cases and experiential exercises are especially useful here for generating class discussion. Questionnaires that assess organizational communication attitudes or behavior are also quite helpful in personalizing the course content for the students. Finally, when the course is taught at the senior level, students are usually very receptive to a treatment of job hunting communication skills, since many of them are interviewing on campus with potential employers or will be soon.

Student evaluations. Because of the survey nature of its scope, this course places relatively little emphasis on the basic skills stressed in the basic business communication class. Consequently, assignments would be graded primarily on content. Obviously, however, language conventions cannot be ignored; and students should be made to realize that their respect for these conventions (or lack thereof) could mean the difference of a grade on their assignments.

For a term project in this course, a teacher might offer a degree of flexibility given the small size of the class. This flexibility might work to maximize the value of the learning experience provided by the project because the student is more likely to be working on something of genuine personal interest. Some of the options that might be offered are primary research, secondary research, an original organizational communication case and its analysis, and a videotaped skit dealing with one of the subjects treated in the course. In the latter case, the student(s) would be expected to present the videotape to the class, along with whatever handout(s) might be appropriate, and lead a class discussion of it.

A student once referred to a course such as the one just described as a class in organizational survival. To the extent that a person's job and career are ultimately governed by his/her ability to interact effectively with others, that student's words may have provided an apt description.

INTERCULTURAL BUSINESS COMMUNICATION

Because of burgeoning world trade during the latter half of this century and because of consequent AACSB recommendations, the field of international business is finding its way into the curriculums of many colleges of business in this country. As was noted earlier in this chapter, some schools are complying with those AACSB recommendations by working the subject of international business into existing courses. Others are creating new courses, with an international focus, in the various functional business area. The following paragraphs will deal with one such new course in intercultural business communication.

Course content. The introduction of a course in intercultural business communication might present a brief history of the development of U.S. world trade over the course of this century. Extensive statistics on the present state of U.S. international trade might be used to impress upon the students the likelihood of their eventual involvement in some aspect of international business. Students might be further convinced of this likelihood if shown the extent of financial involvement in and ownership of "American" firms by foreign investors. All this data could be presented in conjunction with a view of a world that is shrinking due to major advancements in technology and transportation.

A second course section could focus on barriers to effective intercultural communication. Barriers worthy of note would be ethnocentrism, the belief that people are people and business is business everywhere, and culture shock.

The third course section might then be devoted to showing how people differ. It might demonstrate how many beliefs and practices in this country differ from those of most other cultures. It could treat such areas as the relationship of family and friends to business, the pervasiveness of religion, etiquette, individualism versus conformity, presentation organizations and styles, and verbal and nonverbal considerations.

The next course section might focus on the diverse cultural aspects of specific countries with which the United States is most heavily involved in trade. Politics, religion, education, etiquette, traditions, recreation, and family are all topics that could be explored for each country.

Another topic worthy of treatment somewhere in an intercultural business communication course would be communication within a multicultural corporation. Attention here could be given to the media employed, the types and volumes of information needed, and the communication systems employed, as well as how they might be improved.

The conclusion of a course in intercultural business communication could fittingly focus on two worthy goals. The first goal to be faced by any American intercultural business communicator is that of eliminating the stereotype of the not so pretty American held by many people of other cultures. The harmful impression left by many who have gone before can be erased only by a great cultural sensitivity demonstrated by all those who now represent the United States in the world market. If this first goal is achieved, the second should be forthcoming. That second goal is the meeting of worldwide opportunities and challenges. If, however, American business people refuse to be culturally sensitive and insist that people of other nationalities conform to the "American way," they will find that those people will end up directing their trade to other countries that are less demanding and more accommodating.

Course delivery. Very few business communication teachers have traveled extensively enough or have lived abroad for sufficient lengths of time to have become expert on all the subjects treated in the course just described. Reading and other forms of professional development can certainly help one to prepare to teach a course of this nature, but other resources can add still more to the value of the teaching/learning experience.

Guest lecturers can add immeasurably to the authenticity of the subject's treatment. Perhaps well-traveled executives from international business firms would be the ideal resource, but others are available. Foreign students can provide valuable insights into their cultures. American students who have made lengthy visits abroad can likewise provide interesting perspectives. Finally, students might make oral presentations of research into particular countries, perhaps with particular investment opportunities as the focus.

Student evaluations. Only one note will be made on the subject of student evaluations. To encourage foreign students (potentially valuable resources) to enroll in a course on intercultural business communication, a teacher might have to exercise some discretion in his/her evaluation of their use of the English language. Since it is a second language to them, they won't always recognize and apply its idioms. To hold foreign students up to the same language-use standards applied to American students would be to subject them to a grade disadvantage that probably would discourage their enrollment in the course. On the other side of the coin, most teachers of foreign students will testify that these students can rarely be faulted for not trying their best and that they usually submit assignments that are very good in content if not in language technicalities.

BUSINESS RESEARCH METHODS AND REPORTS

The last major course offering to be described here as suitable for a business communication curriculum at a four-year college or university is labeled business research methods and reports. Though described here as one course, it could conceivably be taught as one class in research methods and one in reports.

Course content. If this course is taught at the senior level (two years after the basic business communication class) and if diagnostic testing reveals a need, this class might begin with a review of basic concepts of written and spoken presentations.

Following this foundation might come a segment on defining the research problem and planning the investigation. The importance of getting the problem clearly in mind cannot be overemphasized. The process of planning the investigation would include the task of determining the subdivisions of the larger problem that need to be studied.

A significant portion of a research methods and reports class and the bulk of a separate research methods class would deal with the topic of data collection methods. Secondary research and documentation might be covered with the help of the library staff. Types of primary research might be reviewed in conjunction with reviews of research instrument development and sampling techniques.

The next course section on data tabulation, analysis, and interpretation is another one that would differ between the one-course and two-course approaches. A separate course in business research methods would likely examine the subject of statistical analysis in a good deal more depth than would a single course in research methods and reports. Regardless of the course approach (one or two classes), however, the topic of outlining would be a suitable item for inclusion here. Although the problem subdivisions would provide some structure for the investigation, the finer points of outlining would best be handled after the data has been collected, tabulated, and analyzed.

The last course subsection might appropriately be devoted to report formatting. Report parts and structures might be examined in terms of the options available in the contexts of length and formality. Additionally, writing style and graphic aids would warrant treatment here. All of these subjects might be covered within the framework of the informational, analytical, and persuasive report classification scheme.

Course delivery. In the delivery of a course in business research methods and reports, one feature assumes major importance. Because of the number of oral presentations that students would be making in class and because of the number of written presentations to be graded by the teacher outside of class, class size must be kept small. If at all possible, such a course should not enroll more than 20 students per section.

Evaluation of the students. A course of this nature lends itself to a series of assignments that are interrelated. Ideally, these assignments should be intimately related to each student and his/her career potential. The first assignment might be a corporation analysis. The company chosen should be one that has definite career possibilities for the student. This analysis will serve two purposes. First, it will familiarize the student with the company's past, present, and future and thus better equip the student to approach the company as a candidate for employment. Second, it will acquaint the student with the problems, opportunities, and challenges now facing or soon to face the company.

The student might then choose one of these problems, opportunities, or challenges for further investigation. The second assignment might thus take the form of an annotated bibliography on the subject chosen.

Armed with this additional insight into the problem, opportunity, or challenge, the student could then complete the third assignment. This could be a proposal for secondary and primary research on the topic selected. One could, however, require two separate proposals so that the secondary research could be completed prior to the writing up of the proposal for the primary research. These secondary and primary research projects would then be the fourth and fifth (or fourth and sixth) assignments.

Once the students have familiarized themselves with a company and industry and with the means by which research is done and reported in business, they ought to be ready for the next assignment. More specifically, they ought to be able to evaluate a piece of research—perhaps a research-based business article.

Finally, in the case of any or all of these written assignments, the teacher might have the students make oral presentations of their projects. If class size cannot be kept reasonable, a teacher might consider allowing students with similar career interests to work in small groups for both the written and oral presentations.

CONCLUSION

The business literature contains no shortage of research findings and authoritative statements relating the ability to communicate to career success. Notations of this relationship appear in national professional and popular publications on what sometimes seems like an almost daily basis. Nonetheless, the discipline of communication in a business college setting continues to receive widely divergent degrees of respect from colleagues and administrators. As was noted earlier, the origins of these varied peer reactions are far too involved (and perhaps institutionally unique) for treatment here.

The fact remains, however, that there is a great deal more to communication in business than a review of letters, memos, and reports. Business communicators today must be much more than good writers and speakers. They must be good listeners, and they must be nonverbally sensitive. They must be psychologically attuned to others, and they must be astute organizational politicians. They must be good interviewers and must know how to conduct meetings. They must be able to resolve conflicts with, between, and among others. They have to be able to do whatever research is necessary to solve problems or respond to opportunities and challenges. They should be familiar with the communication technology available to them. In addition, they are very likely to have to represent their companies and country in dealings with people of other cultures.

Realistically preparing students for their communication roles in business could conceivably take a multitude of course offerings. This chapter has described four courses that would represent at least a good start toward equipping students with the communication tools and abilities they will need for career survival and success.

CHAPTER 14

Teaching Communication for Business At the Graduate Level

GRETCHEN N. VIK

San Diego State University, San Diego, California

While business communication courses are somewhat less common at the graduate level, teachers of graduate students are aware that these students need help in developing and polishing their written and oral communication skills. Graduate students need to learn strategies for solving communication problems, how organizational communication works in actual practice, how to make successful oral and written presentations selling themselves and their firm's services, and how to use interpersonal communication skills to improve their score in the game of office politics. Typically, students also need to polish both written and oral skills, to study communication theory, to learn research skills, and to become familiar with technological advances.

This chapter will describe (1) how graduate courses in business communication are currently structured, (2) what a survey of academic and business sources found ought to be included in such courses, (3) how to teach communication skills to graduate students, and (4) how to evaluate student communication skills. Some of the information in this chapter comes from materials published by the American Assembly of Collegiate Schools of Business (AACSB) and the Association for Business Communication (ABC). The AACSB has collected material on existing graduate-level courses in two published notebooks.[1] The ABC Graduate Studies Committee has developed a sample course outline for a semester-long, three-hour, MBA-level business communication course.[2] In addition to these materials, course outlines were gathered from a number of other graduate business programs.

CURRENT GRADUATE COMMUNICATION COURSES

Current graduate communication courses fall into several patterns: a basic required course plus electives; a full program of communication courses leading to a Ph.D. program; elective programs, either courses or workshops; specific courses based on results of proficiency examinations; and inter-

---

[1]Munter, Mary, editor. *Business Communications: Programs and Courses 1982-83.* St. Louis: American Assembly of Collegiate Schools of Business, 1983; and Munter, Mary, editor. *New Directions for Business Communication 1985.* St. Louis: American Assembly of Collegiate Schools of Business, 1985.

[2]ABC Graduate Studies Committee. "A Graduate Business Communication Course Outline." *Bulletin of the Association for Business Communication* 49:30-33; September 1986.

disciplinary or integrated courses, where communication skills are developed as part of a required management, marketing, accounting, finance, or information systems course.

Basic required course plus electives. An example of a core communication course is the one given by the Sloan School of Management at the Massachusetts Institute of Technology (MIT). First offered in 1985-86, it is a separate course running from the middle of the first term until the middle of the second term, but it includes integrated assignments with other core courses. This required course covers writing and speaking skills needed for success in management. Both internal and consulting presentations and writing are included, as are graphics and listening. Large-group lectures are combined with small-group discussions and presentations; individual work can also be arranged.

The electives offered at Sloan School of Management include an advanced managerial communication course, which adds small-group decision making, conducting meetings, media interviews, and other topics to more advanced writing and speaking practices. It also offers special tutorials for foreign students. Integrated assignments with other core courses can also be developed.

Dartmouth's Amos Tuck School of Business Administration has a two-quarter required core course offered the first two quarters of the MBA program. The course covers communication strategy, writing, speaking, and corporate communication. The first term concentrates on communication analysis, strategy, and oral presentation skills, culminating in a project presentation for a managerial economics course. The second term covers writing improvement and corporate communication. The school also offers an advanced second-year elective course.

The University of Utah requires a business report writing class of all two-year MBA's and any one-year MBA's whose undergraduate business degree did not require such a course—about 10 percent. Students write a major paper of publishable quality plus weekly in-class writing assignments on case studies and progress reports on the long paper. They also give two video presentations.

Elective work at the University of Utah includes integrated oral assignments in accounting and management classes. These oral projects involve students' planning the assignments with other course professors, attending workshops or in-class sessions on the assignments, practicing in the media studio, videotaping the presentations, and critiquing their own and their peers' presentations.

Further electives in communication at the University of Utah include Marketing Communication (videotaping with critique), Interpersonal Competence (role-playing with a behaviorist in management and a communication specialist), Interviewing Workshops, and an intensive Teacher Development Seminar for Ph.D. students.

At the Colgate Darden Graduate School at the University of Virginia, students are required to take a two-semester course called Analysis and Communication their first year. Eight written assignments and numerous

5- to 10-minute presentations give students extensive communication practice and help them become aware of what skills successful communication involves. An elective course in writing and speaking is offered when needed to give students more practice in formal presentations, which are required in a number of their other classes.

At the Fuqua School of Business at Duke University, students take one required first-year class in public speaking and concise and clear business writing. Using large lecture sections on principles and small performance sections, the class provides significant practice and critique from peers and professors.

The second-year elective course, Managerial Effectiveness, is an organizational behavior elective focusing on employee relationships. This course uses an assessment center to measure interpersonal abilities. Duke also offers workshops in interviewing and special communication events such as the Public Affairs Symposium.

Full program of communication courses. Few schools have the resources to offer a full program of communication courses. The University of Texas at Austin has nine graduate business communication classes and offers a Ph.D. in organizational/business communication. The eight seminar topics include business and organizational research methodology; career development; nonverbal communication analysis for organizations; problem solving, proposal writing, and oral presentation; the public relations role and function in managerial communication; advanced writing and editing for executives; advanced report writing, professional reports, and other scholarly papers; and information systems management. The ninth course is an individual research project. A further course includes ten rotating topics, such as leadership and interviewing, nonverbal communication, data communication systems, organizational consulting, international business communication, and telecommunication, under the heading Communication Research for Organizations. An MBA emphasis in business communication is possible, and graduate students are encouraged to take communication electives to enhance their programs.

Elective courses or workshops. Many schools address graduate student communication problems through elective courses. At Stanford, the communication skills program offers students workshops and seminars in addition to reviewing papers that students write for two core courses. The workshops involve making presentations, using visuals, appearing on television, writing business documents effectively, and planning productive meetings. Students can also receive individual help in writing and speaking. Interestingly, the business school suggests that students take regularly offered writing and speaking classes in the school of engineering since the business school does not offer them.

Cornell University's Johnson Graduate School of Management offers two seven-week elective courses in management writing and oral communication. Students get intensified, personalized practice in each type of communication because of the small (10-15 students) class size. Other electives offered include a communication tutorial workshop, where students can get help on papers for other courses, job letters, and other oral presentations. To use its facilities fully, the school sponsors a summer management communication course for nonbusiness students and staff and an effective speaking workshop for the Executive Development Program; it also makes faculty videotapes for reviewing teaching methods.

New York University (NYU) offers a three-unit elective course in management communication, as well as two other electives, Communication as Advocacy, and Media Management and Public Affairs. Like many of the graduate schools, NYU uses cases to develop discussion of communication strategies and solutions. The public affairs class alternates speakers with student-led seminars on the same topics the following week.

The University of Michigan has two elective courses in written and oral communication. If a student has not yet taken a business communication class in undergraduate school, the written communication class is required. In addition to these two credit courses, the school offers workshops on interviewing techniques and resume writing and seminars on communication for managers.

Proficiency examinations. Another way of solving the limited resource problem is to use a proficiency exam so that students who most need help can be required to take relevant courses. At Rutgers University students who do not pass the proficiency exam (about 35 percent) must take an 11-week course on business presentation skills, which includes written and oral practice as well as a library research component.

The School of Urban and Public Affairs at Carnegie-Mellon University requires some students to take its management communication courses based on placement tests. Other elective courses offered include public speaking and interview techniques. Other shorter courses are offered in vocal resonance and communication for executives.

Interdisciplinary or integrated courses. Columbia University offers a program of noncredit short courses and tutorials on oral business presentations, writing for business, business writing for nonnatives, and interviewing practice. Videotaping is frequent and critiqued; classes are small (8-15 students); individual help is readily available. Columbia also sponsors a speaking competition (with a cash prize) each term. The short courses can be integrated with material from required core courses.

At Wharton, graduate students have four semesters to be certified as proficient in writing or speaking skills. They may be evaluated in courses, through taking noncredit workshops, or through individual tutoring. The writing and speaking workshops have 10-12 students each to allow for personal instruction. A full elective course in management communication also gives a chance to practice skills while consulting with local firms on communication problems.

These five patterns obviously have some advantages and disadvantages for the schools that use them. A required course plus electives seems to have the widest possible application because it requires all students to study certain fundamental material and gives other choices for later work depending on student needs and inclinations. However, students might choose not to take extra courses because their communication skills are weak, and thus students needing more help would not receive it.

A full program of courses is a wonderful source of electives for students in any business emphasis. The clear disadvantage of this type of program is resource allocation and the accompanying difficulty in finding qualified instructors for such a variety of classes. Many administrations would have trouble finding enough financial support for a full program.

Elective programs are often less expensive to staff because of their flexible nature, and the workshops can also be used to generate more money through executive development programs. But elective programs may not teach all the students who need help, and staff turnover can make consistency difficult.

Using a proficiency examination helps get the most assistance to those who need help, such as part-time or night students.

An integrated program is very desirable so that students see the need for good communication skills in all their classes, but it takes a large amount of development and grading work and is often difficult to implement because so many faculty members are involved.

So what course program is best for graduate students? Obviously it depends on the school's resources and its student population. To expose students to all the skills and topics that faculty members and active business people suggest would mean at least one required course and workshops and seminars as needed, based on a proficiency examination. It is important to look at what the programs investigated have in common.

Through examination of the course syllabus notebooks available from AACSB and course materials obtained from other schools, some commonalities can be observed among the 18 programs studied.

1. All cover both written *and* oral communication. Many of the individual courses include both written and oral communication, while courses and workshops on oral communication alone far outnumber ones solely on written communication.

2. Elective courses and workshops most often include job interviews, public speaking/oral reporting, media interviews and public affairs, interpersonal communication, nonverbal communication, and corporate advocacy.

3. Virtually all of the schools have or have access to a video lab, so students' individual and group presentations can be videotaped and reviewed by students and other evaluators.

4. Most programs include some "real life" component, whether it is cases, business speakers, or presentations to business audiences.

5. Most courses are limited to a small enrollment (20-30 students) so students can receive individual attention. Many of the workshops are even smaller, so students get a lot of feedback on their communication skills.

Some interesting ideas found in single programs are an endowed essay competition for business students (Cornell); a six-week course in vocal resonance (Carnegie-Mellon); encouraging publishing of student work (University of Utah); a course in writing for nonnatives (Columbia); special tutorials for foreign students (MIT); and a speech workshop with Toastmasters (University of Western Ontario). Two schools, University of Texas and Dartmouth, have variable topic electives on advanced communication topics such as oral presentations, written software documentation, and telecommunication.

The 18 programs studied include, for the most part, the topics recommended by the business/academic survey discussed next.

COURSE SYLLABUS BASED ON FACULTY/BUSINESS SURVEY

The 1984-1985 Graduate Studies Committee of the Association for Business Communication surveyed recent MBA's and executive development course participants to discover topics that should be included in a graduate communication course. The survey results, reported in the September 1986 issue of *The Bulletin of the Association for Business Communication*, agreed for the most part with faculty perceptions of topic importance. Based on these results, the committee compiled the following syllabus for a three-hour, semester-long, MBA-level core business communication course.

Section 1: Written Communication. The Writing Process, Business Writing, Condensed and Abbreviated Documents, Argumentation, Graphics, Directives, Extemporaneous Writing, Briefing Technique

Section 2: Oral Communication. Internal Speaking, Meetings, Interviews, Listening, Media Confrontations, Rhetorical Considerations

Section 3: Communication Theory and Concepts. Communication Theory, Communication Strategies, Interpersonal Communication, Organization Communication, Information Theory, Metacommunication, Media, Nonverbal Communication, Language and Culture

Section 4: Technology. Information Technology, Word Processing, Communication Technology

Section 5: Business Orientations. Ethics, Corporate Advocacy

Section 6: Research. Research Overview, Organizing the Research Investigation, Statistical Design and Analysis for Survey Research[3]

This syllabus includes the topics considered most important by both faculty and business practitioners, with emphasis as follows.

Written Communication. This section covers the writing process from planning to revision, formats and types of documents (reports, memos, proposals, letters, summaries), writing to persuade, and writing to inform. Because the basics of written communication strategy also underlie oral communication, this first section of the syllabus would probably be allotted a fairly large block of time, especially at schools where students have little prior experience in business writing.

Oral Communication. In oral communication, emphasis is on internal speaking, meetings, and interviews, with an added section on listening and one on media confrontation. Note that making formal speeches to outside groups was not considered common enough to include as a course topic. The internal speaking topics all deal with presentations: presentations to peers,

---

[3]*Ibid.*, 32-33.

executive committees, and boards of directors and on how to organize and deliver the presentation. The interview topics include both employment and appraisal types.

This section gives an extensive overview of the oral communication topics a graduate student needs to be familiar with and could serve as an outline for a complete course, as could the written communication section. With a video lab and relatively small classes, an instructor could cover this material and have students practice a number of kinds of speech experiences.

Communication Theory and Concepts. This section on audience analysis, interpersonal and organizational communication, metacommunication, nonverbal communication, and intercultural communication could be handled with readings, discussion, and student speeches or short written reports. Integrating the content areas of the syllabus into the application parts would make it possible to cover all the material in a three-unit semester course.

Technology. So that students are prepared for the offices where they will go to work, the sample syllabus includes a quick overview of information and communication technology, such as commonly used software and telecommunications. Some of these topics would make good speech and research topics. Others, like word processing or telecommunications, could be logically integrated into the written and oral communication sections.

Business Orientations. Ethics and corporate advocacy would again make good research and presentation topics.

Research. Depending on whether graduate students receive further instruction on research, this syllabus section could be expanded into an entire class, a short course, or a unit of instruction.

Since this syllabus is quite comprehensive, it could easily become the basis of at least three communication courses: one in written communication, one in oral communication, and one in theory and research. Because many schools are only able to begin a graduate program, the three-unit overview course was suggested as a foundation course on which to build later. The syllabus is similar to that currently in use in many undergraduate programs, so it is possible to cover all the topics in one semester, especially with advanced students who have some business experience.

The course outline does not include methods of teaching the various topics, but the committee compiled bibliographies on the various topics as a beginning list of helpful sources for instructors. The technology topic, of course, will have to be updated constantly by the instructor through the use of periodicals, vendor literature, and possibly business/vendor speakers in class.

METHODS OF TEACHING COMMUNICATION SKILLS
TO GRADUATE STUDENTS

Because many graduate students are older and have been in the business world for a few years already, some appropriate teaching methods are similar to those used in industrial training. Such methods include videotaping, small-group work, role-playing, guest speakers, and case analysis.

Certainly lecture and discussion are still valid methods for teaching content segments of the courses, but the very nature of communication means that students learn best about successful communication techniques by actually practicing and applying the principles they are reading about. The fact that many graduate students have work experience since completing their undergraduate degrees also tends to make these students very pragmatic about how useful course information will be to them. Thus, for example, case histories seem more relevant than theory without such anecdotes.

Videotaping. As noted earlier, virtually every program investigated uses a video lab for at least part of the oral communication section of the course. The advantages of videotaping include more flexible scheduling (rather than using a large chunk of class time, students can have speeches taped independently), more detailed peer and professor critiques because of having a tape to watch, and of course, the chance for speakers to evaluate their own performance.

Equipment cost and administrative details such as scheduling are possible problem areas with videotaping, but these possible disadvantages are usually outweighed by the strong advantages. In addition to videotaping speeches and question-and-answer sessions such as press conferences, some classes videotape mock job interviews, guest speakers, and panel discussions so students can view them more than once or for self-evaluation or peer evaluation.

Small-group work. Written and oral presentations in the business world are frequently done by small groups or teams, so it is logical to make written and oral assignments to be performed in small groups (usually four to six students). A group oral presentation can be graded on structure, visual aids, and presentation skills. A team-written report can be graded on the same points as an individual report, of course.

Small groups can also practice interpersonal communication skills such as are needed in department meetings, briefing sessions, board meetings, and press conferences. A typical group oral assignment would be a group analysis of an industry or a panel seminar on a previous guest speaker's topic, with a group-written report on the seminar topic made available to the class before the panel presentation.

Small groups can also be used for peer evaluation of either written or oral work and for case analysis study groups before class discussion of cases.

Role-playing. Role-playing is particularly common in teaching interviewing skills, and videotaping gives all the players a chance to review their own performance as well as that of others. A common training technique, role-playing gives students a nonthreatening way to practice confrontation and negotiation skills as well as other interpersonal skills.

Guest speakers. Some ideas for guest speakers include a guest lecturer from Toastmaster International conducting workshops on impromptu speaking; a panel on office politics, including managers, organizational behavior experts, and communication consultants; and speakers from local corporations speaking on public affairs issues confronting managers. At Arizona State University students write a report critiquing the organization and style of three business executives' oral presentations. This is one way students can develop the listening skills that are the oral counterpart of the editing skills they learn in evaluating their own and others' writing.

Case analysis. Cases are often used to illustrate issues in corporate communication. Students can be asked to analyze and solve the communication problem orally or in writing. Having case details to work with helps students analyze their audience and determine how to approach the solution.

A further advantage of using cases is that they tend to give students more information about how businesses operate, which will help them become more successful managers. Cases are particularly good for illustrating problems of negotiation or of interpersonal conflicts and can be used for role-play to further investigate these situations. Cases can also be used as exams to determine if students can reach and explain logical conclusions from the facts given in the cases.

Possible assignments for more traditional methods. Some interesting assignments noted in various course outlines might serve as suggestions to graduate instructors.

WRITTEN COMMUNICATION. Incorporate real-world assignments, such as having students produce job-search correspondence; abstract an article for a busy executive; analyze and write a report on graphics; or report on a short library research assignment on a person, company, or product. Some interesting sample assignments from Cornell include:

- Explain a concept, theory, process, apparatus, policy, or product to new employees or new students who have a need to know about it.
- Identify and evaluate a few of the major new trends (regulatory, competitive, technological) that are affecting the field or industry in which you plan to work. Why are they important? Are the results positive or negative? Are they likely to persist? What should be done to encourage, reverse, or accommodate them?
- Assume you are a management trainee who has returned to work and found nine different writing tasks from your supervisor. Arrange them in order of importance and then complete as many as possible in 1¼ hours.

ORAL COMMUNICATION. Oral communication activities could include presenting a ceremonial speech; explaining something technical to a lay audience; giving an informative speech with required visual aids; researching and explaining a topic; persuading a particular hostile audience; presenting major findings of a paper written for another class; simulating a one-hour television interview; defending a formal business plan; and serving as master of ceremonies for a speech class—arranging format, checking on speakers, getting equipment.

The overall intent of such realistic assignments for written and oral communication students is to give practice in solving problems students will soon face. A course description from Tulane University even describes the course as similar to a training seminar, telling students to imagine that they are members of management involved in decision making.

How methods work with major syllabus topics. The most common methods used in the analyzed course outlines can be grouped as lecture-discussion and critiquing papers and speeches. Typically a writing class is about half lecture-discussion and half critiquing papers, while a speaking class might be one-third each—lecture-discussion, speeches, and critiquing speeches. The ABC sample syllabus discussed earlier would logically use application and critique for most of the written and oral sections and lecture-discussion for the theory, technology, business orientations, and research sections. Interestingly enough, most course outlines examined contained a page on production specifications for papers, as students have little typing or publication background.

Depending on the student population, schools (like Wharton) may offer intensive workshops or special course sections for foreign students. Tulane's foreign student course acts as an orientation to American culture as well as giving practice in writing and presenting business reports and using computer software. Similar intensive courses for students scoring low on proficiency tests use traditional methods for upgrading skills, including lots of application after lectures and discussion on the theory.

Another method used in a number of programs, as mentioned earlier, is to integrate communication skills training into other classes. In these integrated classes, the method of actually teaching the communication skills is usually team teaching, with a communication professor doing lectures, grading, and critiquing for that segment of the course. A field study similarly integrates communication skills with material being learned about the functional areas.

EVALUATING STUDENT COMMUNICATION SKILLS

Since communication skills are mostly judged by how well they work when applied, evaluating communication skills has to be, for the most part, a subjective process.

Grading breakdowns. Here are some sample grading breakdowns from the course outlines for a written communication class: in-class preparation, readings, and discussion, 50 percent; homework and short paper, 25 percent; final paper, 25 percent. Another written communication class uses these breakdowns: written assignments, 25 percent; rewrites, 25 percent; research project, 25 percent; class participation and discussion, 25 percent. For an oral communication class, these breakdowns are used: individual oral presentations, 40 percent; group oral presentations, 40 percent; class participation (peer evaluations) and homework, 20 percent. For a combined written and oral communication class the breakdowns are written exercises, 20 percent; two individual papers, 30 percent; group paper, 10 percent; two oral presentations, 20 percent; class participation, 20 percent. For a public relations class, these are the breakdowns: term paper, 40 percent; participation, discussion, three-page preliminary paper, 25 percent; final short answer and essay examination, 35 percent.

One interesting point about almost all the course outlines is that attendance is mentioned. While this might seem very structured for a graduate class, it is easy to see that makeups on case analysis, guest speakers, and application-type in-class assignments in writing and speaking would be nearly impossible to schedule.

A few course outlines specifically mention that the course will be graded pass/fail. These courses tend to focus on skill development through practice and to have small numbers of students—15 for writing and 10 for speaking classes—to allow for individual attention.

Evaluating written work. All the course outlines for written communication classes mention how class work will be evaluated, but the criteria are subjective rather than objective. In addition to requiring standard usage (syntax, grammar, mechanics, diction), schools list the following as expected basic skills: coherence, completeness, strategy, logic, evidence, critical reading and thinking, credibility, structure, voice, control of language, style, concern for audience, appropriate tone, precise language, and a professionalism in strategy and format.

In evaluating case analysis, course outlines require that students comprehend and abstract information from business cases or documents in addition to basic written and oral communication skills. Schools with combined courses or theory sections in their course outlines tend also to ask for conceptual ability, interpersonal communication skills, and a higher level of strategy skills.

Evaluating oral presentations. According to the evaluation forms included in several course outlines, oral presentations are evaluated along traditional lines, by content, delivery, and use of visuals. Content, of course, includes planning, timing, providing appropriate depth and wealth of topics, and using examples. Delivery covers eye contact, stance, gestures, movement, energy level, and use of notes. Visual use includes timing, appropriateness, and readability.

Evaluating group work. When students produce written reports or oral presentations as a group of four to seven, evaluation becomes more complex. One way of handling group projects is to give each student the same grade, but this may penalize the best students and give something of a free ride to students not producing their share of the work.

Another way to grade group projects is to use peer evaluation, either cooperatively or individually. In the first instance, the group meets, divides points according to individual input on the project, and all members sign off on the grading form. (If the report gets 80 percent and four people worked on it, they have 320 points to divide. No one can get more than 100 points.) The difficulty with this method occurs when one student, rated very low by the group, refuses to sign off on the form.

Individual peer evaluations produce confidential evaluations of comparative group work that are then averaged or otherwise combined by the instructor.

Evaluating graduate work. From these lists of grading points and methods, it is obvious that evaluating graduate work is similar to evaluating any student work in communication. Basic skills may be assumed (but will not always be present) so that teachers can spend more time on communication theory and application of higher level skills. However, some students will still have to be judged on their inadequate preparation in earlier education. To avoid seeming to grade on minutiae, teachers can emphasize how "inconspicuous style" (which has no distractions of spelling, punctuation, diction, mechanics, or syntax) helps communicate a message best.

CONCLUSION

Graduate communication classes need to be included in graduate business programs so that students can be adequately prepared for the work they will do upon graduation. An ideal program would have initial courses in written and oral communication to brush up on skills, to become familiar with business formats, and to practice communication in these formats. Later courses would cover interpersonal communication and office politics, organizational communication and public relations, business-media relations, information technology, ethics, crisis communication, interviewing from both sides of the desk, answering questions as a speaker, editing subordinates' work, using visuals, and impromptu speaking. Until this ideal is reached (when time, resources, and staff are infinite, and students come to school with a good foundation in basic skills), graduate schools will continue to offer a judicious combination of regular courses, short courses, workshops, and labs, and will try to cover the whole range of communication skills needs in the courses they can offer.

Some trends noted at the November 1986 Association for Business Communication panel on graduate education include the following:

- Writing instruction is moving toward communication strategies and away from emphasis on type of document.
- Speaking courses are becoming more common, with the emphasis on presentations rather than speeches.
- Visuals are emphasized more, with video, computer graphics, and desktop publishing options.
- Oral presentations are growing out of written assignments rather than being generated separately.
- More courses are offered in interpersonal communication, advocacy, corporate cultures, and public relations (media, image, crisis communication).
- Courses are considering the global environment, cultural barriers, and internationalism more than in the past.
- Research on managerial communication issues is used as topics for writing and speaking.
- Information technology is another fertile research area.

Current courses have many desirable features to copy, and the future appears promising as administrators begin to realize the importance of good communication skills to the success of their graduates.

Part V

CONCLUSION: A TIME FOR ACTION

CHAPTER 15

Facilitating Communication for Business

JAMES CALVERT SCOTT
Utah State University, Logan

Communication skills are essential for success. Of all the personal and professional characteristics that enhance people's chances of getting ahead, none consistently ranks of higher importance than the ability to communicate, the capacity to react to and interact with others. At the same time, while communication skills are widely acknowledged as requisites for success, numerous speakers and writers have expressed concern about the communication skills that many people have.

Business students and workers have borne the brunt of much of the criticism. Researchers in study after study of business students, graduates, and employees have noted serious deficiencies in communication skills for business. Furthermore, business executives continue to report the discrepancy between the low level of business communication skills found in the workplace and the high level of business communication skills needed there. While business educators have commendably taught the technical skills of business, they have been less successful in teaching the communication skills for business. Consequently, many of those preparing to enter and those already employed in business occupations are ill-equipped for success because of their limited communication proficiencies.

Communication skills are important for success on personal and professional levels. As people develop and refine various communication skills, they strengthen perceptions of their capabilities. Armed with growing confidence in basic communication skills, people are better able to achieve their personal goals. On the professional level, people who are hired nowadays no longer possess just the necessary technical skills of business; they must also possess the ability to communicate effectively in a variety of business circumstances. Business workers are also encouraged to continue to refine their current communication skills and to add new ones to increase their complement of skills for business purposes. Consequently, the ability to communicate well is rapidly becoming the requisite for promotion in the business world.

Furthermore, the success or failure of all business functions depends on communication skills. Employees in different functional areas of business must coordinate their efforts. Only when appropriate two-way communication flows among the people responsible for such divergent business functions as producing, marketing, managing, and accounting can businesses be successful.

151

ACCEPTING THE RESPONSIBILITIES

Business educators have responsibilities for teaching communication skills for business since they tend to be better prepared to do so than representatives of other groups. By virtue of both their academic coursework in business communication and related disciplines and their practical experiences while employed in business occupations, business educators understand the importance of possessing—and actually possess—the communication skills for business. Having both theoretical and applied experiences, business educators overall possess more balanced preparation for providing relevant business communication skill instruction than members of other groups.

Responsibilities for the teaching of communication skills for business must rest with all business educators regardless of their areas of specialization or levels of instruction. Because of the wide diversity of communication skills for business that students and business workers must develop, all business educators must participate; the task is too large and too complex to be achieved by only some business educators. While only selected business educators will teach classes called Business Communication or some related name, other business educators can do much to help. They can emphasize to their students the importance of developing a wide variety of communication skills for business, utilize activities in their classrooms that develop and refine communication skills as they teach in their own areas of specialization, and support the efforts of their colleagues to advance communication skills. With all business educators coordinating their efforts, the communication skills of business students and workers can be strengthened.

The goal of improving the business communication skills of students and workers is challenging but achievable. To reach that goal, business educators of all types at all instructional levels must accept these basic responsibilities: (1) understand the foundations of business communication, (2) develop specializations that strengthen communication skill instruction, and (3) teach relevant business communication skills in all assigned courses. In addition, business educators who specialize in the business communication area must accept other responsibilities. They must conduct needed business communication research and other scholarly activities, train others to teach business communication content effectively, provide training programs for employees of businesses, and offer consultative services to help businesses resolve their communication problems. Only when business educators en masse accept significant responsibilities for business communication skill development can it accurately be said that business educators are facilitating communication for business.

UNDERSTANDING THE FOUNDATIONS

Business educators must understand the foundations of business communication, the core components that undergird the discipline. Among these basic but essential parts are the fundamental communication skills of listening, speaking, writing, and reading and organizational communication theory.

Listening skills. Listening skills are vital basic skills for everyone. In fact, experts estimate that people typically should spend nearly half of their communicating time listening, actively involved in the communication process by determining the source of information upon which to focus, by receiving that information through the physical process of hearing, and by manipulating the message symbols to yield meaning. While listening skills are widely recognized as important for both personal and professional development, most people receive little or no formal instruction in listening. As a result, students and businesspersons alike tend to be ineffective listeners who typically function at about 25 percent efficiency according to researchers.

All business educators have responsibilities for teaching listening skills so that their students not only can acquire classroom information for and about business but also can develop appropriate listening skills for successful business employment. Through a variety of learning activities in every class, business educators should emphasize such aspects of listening as understanding the context in which the listening occurs, knowing the characteristics of the listening channel, minimizing as much communication interference as possible, interpreting the meaning of the message in terms of factors influencing the situation, exchanging feedback, and monitoring the degree of communication success. In addition, business educators should teach and positively reinforce throughout the entire business curriculum the use of specific techniques that increase listening proficiency. Obviously there are many opportunities to build listening skills in every business course, and every business educator ought to take full advantage of them.

Speaking skills. Speaking skills are another of the foundations of business communication. In terms of the amount of time that people devote to various types of communication skills, speaking skills rank slightly behind listening skills. People frequently select speaking skills as the most effective means of transmitting information in both educational and work settings.

Business educators ought to be familiar with a variety of speaking skills and proficient in those that have frequent applications in learning and working environments. In many cases business educators have already developed and refined relevant speaking skills through required undergraduate speech courses and through a variety of experiences at work.

Business educators ought to infuse these types of speaking-related topics into their instruction for and about business: basic principles and techniques of speaking, visual and aural dimensions of speaking, forms of support for ideas, organization of ideas, effects of language on ideas and listeners, speaking to inform, speaking to persuade, communicating with groups, and techniques of interviewing.

Since many students respond favorably to different types of speaking activities, business educators can easily use them with content material to build speaking skills for later professional employment. For example, after business correspondence students have written reports, their teachers could have them present the reports as oral briefings to groups of peers, which discuss the reports and vote either to accept or to reject them. Teachers of business dynamics could have their students investigate different career options and then present brief informative speeches that report key findings. Business law teachers might assist students in building persuasive speaking skills through mock trials or debates that are followed by critiques. Teachers of vocational classes might have senior students interview each other for entry-level positions for which they soon will be applying. Opportunities for developing relevant speaking skills in business classes are nearly limitless; business educators should use them frequently.

Writing skills. Writing skills are a significant component of basic communication skills, and people have long regarded them as essential for success in school and in the professions. Of all the basic skills of communication, writing instruction receives the most attention in grades one through twelve. Students at higher educational levels typically continue to prepare for careers in business occupations by enrolling in several additional writing-related courses, including at least one that focuses on business writing.

Business educators should build on the basic writing proficiencies that their students have previously developed. They should focus attention away from literary-style writing and toward business-style writing, keeping in mind that both styles share many elements in common. While developing writing skills, business educators may want to include such topics as a review of basic writing and language mechanics concepts and how to organize, write, edit, and format a variety of types of business letters, business reports, and employment communications.

Writing activities, like speaking activities, can easily be incorporated into instructional strategies by business educators. Since writing is a complex task, all business educators—not just business communication teachers—must work cooperatively to strengthen the business writing skills of students. Some type of writing should be required from students in every business class. Business educators should evaluate that writing against business standards for such factors as content, organization, language mechanics, and format. Students should receive individualized oral or written constructive criticism so that they know what was done well and what needs to be done better in future writing activities. Only when students regularly receive feedback about how they have developed and presented their messages will they learn how to refine their business writing skills. Fortunately, business educators have numerous circumstances in which relevant writing skills can be integrated with business subject matter.

Reading skills. Basic reading skills are another foundation of business communication. As people rise from entry-level positions within business organizations, they spend more time reading both internally and externally generated business communications and need increasingly sophisticated reading skills.

The development of basic reading skills receives a major block of time in elementary and middle school grades, but as a matter of fact, beyond that instructional level most formalized reading courses end. As a result, teachers at higher instructional levels must teach those reading skills that are necessary in order for students to master the subject matter. To assist teachers with that task, many states require teachers to complete a reading methods course before they qualify for initial certification or renewal of certification. Consequently, many business educators have some understanding of the reading process, reading rates and abilities of students, and strategies for developing reading skills in business classes. Business educators are discovering that they can improve student performance in business classes by infusing reading skill instruction with business content. Since many of these same reading skills have direct transfer to reading tasks in the business world, there are double benefits from teaching reading skills in business classes.

All business teachers should strive to strengthen the reading skills of their students, thus contributing to their success now in school and later in business careers. At the minimum, business educators should teach these broad types of reading skills to their students: a method of reading and studying such as SQ3R; word recognition and vocabulary development skills; comprehension skills, including critical reading skills; and adjustment of reading rates to suit varying purposes for reading, types of reading materials, and familiarity with reading topics. For example, the accounting teacher should emphasize the development of vocabulary skills, especially for technical words and common words that also have specialized accounting meanings. The teacher of economic principles might have students read and react to material about economic concepts not only by pointing out the strengths and weaknesses of the writer's presentation but also by making personal value judgments about the presentation. The clerical office skills instructor could teach students how to skim—to read quickly for an overview—and how to scan—to locate specific pieces of information quickly. Both are part of the process of developing flexible reading rates and necessary skills for using records systems efficiently. Opportunities for developing reading skills in business courses do exist and can advance communication skills for business if business educators will take advantage of them.

Organizational communication theory. Business educators need to understand the principles of organizational communication theory. Central to organizational communication is the idea that people in organizations have positional roles that control how they communicate with others. In essence, employees become the kinds of communicators that their organizations compel them to be; freely chosen behavior is possible only if employees are willing to accept the consequences of their actions.

Insights into the complex relationships involving people and organizations are rooted in the classical, behavioral, and systems theories of organizations. They are developed and refined through study of such major topics as information flows, managerial and leadership styles, motivation, organizational communication relationships, styles of communication, communication climate, group processes, communication systems and their influences on messages, communication policies, and communication audits.

Such intertwined but diverse subject matter allows business educators ample opportunities for developing the basic tenets of organizational communication theory. For example, the office procedures teacher might discuss with the class what information is communicated in the office environment, how it is communicated, and to whom it is communicated. The marketing teacher could build concepts relating to motivation and persuasion and discuss how they affect communication. Advisors of business student organizations could develop both the experiential and theoretical aspects of group dynamics by linking occurrences within organizational activities to group dynamics phenomena. Teachers of business principles and management might use activities that develop student understanding of the influence of leadership and managerial styles on communication in the business world. Yes, opportunities do exist for all types of business educators at various instructional levels to infuse organizational communication concepts into their regular subject matter if they are willing to do so.

There are many ways in which all kinds of business educators can incorporate the foundations of business communication—the basic skills of listening, speaking, writing, and reading and organizational communication theory—into their subject matter. Doing so on concerted and consistent bases by accepting responsibilities for the teaching of these foundations will surely be useful in facilitating communication for business.

DEVELOPING COMMUNICATION SPECIALIZATIONS

Business educators must also develop specializations that strengthen the communication skill instruction they provide. Obviously there are many specializations that can do so. Among the more important ones are those that allow business educators to minimize communication apprehension, to build communication skills with technologies, to increase communication skills of nonnative speakers of English, and to develop intercultural communication skills for the global business community.

Minimizing communication apprehension. Many students experience communication apprehension, a sometimes vague but typically obsessive anticipation or fear that creates anxiety when someone thinks about or is actually involved in a communication activity. Some of its symptoms such as beads of sweat on a furrowed brow or trembling may be obvious to even casual observers; others such as a slightly odd feeling may be barely discernible to those who are afflicted. Some people experience communication apprehension from thinking about something that is associated with a communication activity such as a requirement to use an unfamiliar computer graphics package to create pie charts for a report; others experience it from a particular communication activity such as speaking before a group. Some people who experience communication apprehension verbalize their anxieties; others do not. Communication apprehension in all of its variant forms and intensities is an everyday phenomenon that interferes with the development of communication skills for business, one that all business teachers need to be able to address.

There are a variety of strategies that business educators can use to minimize communication apprehension. An important one is to acknowledge the universality of communication apprehension; sooner or later everyone has it. Having communication apprehension does not doom a person to failure forever. Business educators can lay the foundation for rehabilitation by developing caring student-teacher relationships. In addition, business educators should create supportive learning environments that bolster the self-confidence of those who are anxious. Frequent expressions of confidence can overcome self-fulfilling negative anticipations and fears and help to regenerate positive attitudes. Business educators may also find that the technique of shaping behavior, positively rewarding behavior that comes closer and closer to the desired behavior, is useful in overcoming communication apprehension. By taking such supportive actions, business educators can minimize communication apprehension in their classrooms.

Building communication skills with technologies. Technology is changing rapidly, especially in the communication-related areas. Applications that seemed like dreams only a few years ago are reality today. Technology offers faster, more efficient means of communicating. It offers promises for building communication skills as well as some pitfalls.

The basic foundations of communication will remain the same, but technology will change the manner in which and speed with which communication occurs. As a tool of and for communication, technology can both simplify and complicate communication. For example, for a person who possesses advanced word processing skills, a microcomputer can simplify and speed the recording, editing and revising, and formatting steps; for a person who possesses limited word processing skills, a microcomputer can complicate and slow down these steps. The challenge facing teachers is to gain the benefits but not the detriments from technology while building communication skills. Additional research is needed to identify the most effective ways of integrating technology with communication skills.

Technology is a tool of rather than a substitute for communication instruction. As a tool, technology must be subordinated to communication instruction itself by business communication teachers; yet technology should not be ignored since it is increasingly being used to facilitate communication. Time in business communication classes should be spent actively learning the communication processes rather than such technological applications as word processing, computer graphics, and the like. A logical and necessary prerequisite for business communication instruction is a computer-usage class with emphasis on business applications, especially word processing. Having such a prerequisite would allow business communication teachers to focus their attentions on developing communication skills; other business educators could focus their attentions on the gamut of technology-related applications. With coordinated efforts, both groups can contribute toward building better communication skills with technologies.

Increasing communication skills of nonnative speakers. The presence of nonnative speakers of English in the classroom typically causes concern. Teachers wonder if and how they can rise to the additional challenges of teaching subject matter to learners with less than native English proficiency. Students, native and nonnative alike, wonder if their educational needs can reasonably be met as they compete for instructional assistance.

Nonnative speakers of English need caring teachers and supportive environments in which to develop their listening, speaking, writing, and reading skills

157

in English. Nonnatives seem to develop communication skills in English best when their teachers are people-oriented, open-minded, interested in and tolerant of other cultures, fluent in languages, and adaptable. Until nonnative speakers of English become functionally literate in English, perhaps their best interests are served by learning English and other subjects in special classes; once English literacy is attained, they may be mainstreamed with native speakers of English.

If English as a second language classes are available, business educators ought to be certain that their nonnative students have enrolled in them to build as much prior English language competence as is possible. Business educators should encourage nonnative speakers of English to participate actively in the classroom, and they should monitor such students' understanding closely to ensure content mastery. If business educators devote extra attention to vocabulary and concept development activities in their classes, they can increase comprehension of nonnative and native speakers alike. Tutoring by carefully selected classmates and working with skilled native speakers of English on some assignments may also benefit nonnative speakers, as should extra teacher assistance. Business educators should challenge nonnative speakers of English to meet communication standards that at the end of their educational programs are similar to—if not identical to—those for native speakers of English; having significantly lower standards for nonnative speakers than for native speakers is not in the long-term best interest of nonnative speakers of English. Business educators should also realize that although nonnative speakers of English typically require special instructional assistance, they can enrich the learning environment by sharing their unique experiences and viewpoints with their classmates.

Developing intercultural communication skills. As residents of various countries increasingly depend on those of other countries for many of the goods and services they consume, an economically interdependent global business community emerges. To operate efficiently, such a community needs to be staffed by workers who, among other things, are skilled in intercultural communication. These workers ought to understand the effects of cultural factors on beliefs, values, attitudes, and views of themselves and their worlds. Furthermore, they should understand how cultural factors influence all communicators.

When people preparing to work in an intercultural environment receive appropriate instruction, they can minimize "ugly American" behavior, which is typical of persons who are ill-prepared to interact with other cultures. Instruction focusing on such major topics as verbal and nonverbal (including time, space, and gesture) interaction across cultures, understanding of other cultures, and behaviors that prevent and promote effective communication can help to make learners more aware of the many dimensions of intercultural communication.

There are a variety of ways in which business educators can develop intercultural communication skills. For example, foreign-born members of any business class can share their perspectives on any subject, pointing out how and why their perspectives may be different from those of their

American-born classmates. Foreign nationals might be invited to speak to students studying economics to develop insights about the cultures, life-styles, and economic and governmental systems in their countries. People who have worked in other countries might be invited to business law and business principles and management classes to discuss the legal systems and business environments in those countries. Analyses of different writing styles and patterns that are found in written communications prepared by nonnative speakers of English could be used in business communication classes to shed light on beliefs, values, and attitudes that are prevalent in other cultures. Yes, intercultural communication skills can be developed by business educators as they teach regular business content.

By developing relevant specializations, business educators can strengthen the communication skill instruction they provide. As business educators learn how to minimize communication apprehension, they will create more supportive environments in which learners can develop their communication-related skills. Business educators can also learn how to utilize the promises of technologies to build communication skills while also minimizing the corresponding pitfalls. They can also implement strategies that will foster the development of the communication skills of nonnative speakers of English. In addition, business educators can encourage the attainment of the intercultural communication skills that will be required for full participation in the evolving global business community. As business educators develop specializations such as these, they will truly be facilitating communication for business.

TEACHING COMMUNICATION SKILLS

All business educators at various instructional levels must teach relevant business communication skills in their assigned courses. Before they can do so, of course, they must develop an awareness of the current communication skill needs of businesses. Then business educators can infuse appropriate business communication concepts and applications throughout the business curriculum. In addition, selected business educators must accept responsibilities for teaching specialized business communication courses.

Developing an awareness. All business educators must develop an awareness of the current communication skill needs of businesses if they are to provide instruction that facilitates communication for business. They can learn more about current business communication skill needs by reading and studying. The business, business education, and communication literatures include a number of worthwhile articles and books about business communication, and business educators can glean invaluable information from these resources. In addition, enrollment in workshops, seminars, and courses can help business educators develop current and balanced perspectives about the communication skill needs in businesses.

Business educators should maintain active membership in professional organizations of education and business. Among organizations that have taken a variety of actions to support business communication skill development are the National Business Education Association, Delta Pi Epsilon, and the Association for Business Communication. In addition, participation by business educators in selected activities of the organizational communication divisions of such groups as the International Association of Business Communicators, the International Communication Association, and the Speech Communication Association could contribute toward a better understanding of some aspects of business communication. Business educators can learn more about the business perspective on communication skills through certain activities of such organizations as the Academy of Management, the American Management Association, the American Society for Training and Development, and the Public Relations Society of America.

Business educators can also learn much about business communication through interaction with businesspersons and the business community. Those who are affiliated with vocational programs can gather insightful perceptions about communication skills in businesses from the members of their advisory committees. These and other business practitioners have firsthand knowledge about the business communication skills needed for success and about the strengths and weaknesses of the communication skills of recently hired and long-time business workers. Furthermore, business educators themselves can make their own personal assessments of the state of communication skills in businesses as they work in business positions, supervise students participating in cooperative work experience and internship programs, and provide consultative services for businesses. There are, simply stated, a number of ways in which business educators can develop an awareness of the communication skill needs of businesses.

Infusing communication skills. All business educators should infuse business communication concepts and applications throughout their teaching. No part of the curriculum for and about business should be void of activities that develop communication skills. In fact, the infusion of relevant communication skill instruction into business courses can facilitate the subject matter mastery of students. Furthermore, that infusion multiplies the number of vehicles that business educators have for developing personal and professional communication-related knowledges, skills, and attitudes.

Business educators need to consider a variety of factors as they infuse business communication skills throughout the curriculum. First, the integration of business content and communication skills must be orderly and planned. Business educators must communicate with each other to devise coordinated approaches that strengthen the communication skills of students while complementing subject matter mastery. Second, business educators must realistically assess their abilities to teach communication skills; they should build on their areas of strength and take appropriate actions to remedy their areas of weakness. Third, business educators must consider the characteristics of their students. Communication skills should be infused when they are relevant for learners, and the skills should be developed and reinforced in simple-to-complex progressions. Fourth, business educators must utilize effective teaching strategies. Determining how to get maximum benefits from infused communication skill instruction with minimal investments of teaching time and other resources is a challenge that must be addressed. Fifth, business educators must consider constraints realistically when formulating plans. They should have no illusions about faculties, facilities, and finances. All things considered, the infusion of communication skills throughout the business curriculum is one viable approach for strengthening communication skills for business.

Teaching specialized courses. In addition, selected business educators must accept responsibilities for teaching separate business communication courses that are designed to provide instruction about the communication processes that are operational in the business environment. These business communication specialists should have significant interest and skill in communication for business as evidenced by their in-depth academic background in business communication and related disciplines and their proficient demonstrations of communication skills in educational and business settings. Teachers of business communication courses ought to serve as role models for students, fellow business educators, and businesspersons alike.

The content of business communication courses will vary depending on such factors as the grade level placement, the amount of instructional time, and the philosophical orientations of schools, administrators, and faculties. Typical units of instruction in traditional business communication courses focus on these types of topics: basic concepts of writing; language usage and mechanics; and letter, report, and employment communication writing. More diversified and less traditional courses could focus on some or all of these additional topics: intrapersonal, interpersonal, and organizational communication theory; listening skills; speaking skills; reading skills; reference and research skills; problem-solving and decision-making skills; and communication technologies.

Business communication teachers use a variety of instructional and evaluative methods when teaching their courses. Often such methods as assigned readings; instructor or guest lectures; small- and large-group discussions; audiovisual presentations; experiential exercises; listening, speaking, writing, and reading drills and reviews; case problems; role-playing; and coaching, counseling, or conferencing are used to stimulate student interest in and learning of business communication content. Business educators ought to evaluate student mastery in terms of demonstrated communication knowledges, skills, and attitudes that are necessary for successful on-the-job performance in relevant business occupations. Needless to say, the teaching of specialized courses is another viable approach for developing communication skills for business.

All business educators must contribute to communication skill development by teaching those communication skills that are needed in the business world. A two-pronged approach to teaching ought to be used to ensure the development of adequate proficiencies in communication skills for business: infusion of relevant communication skills throughout the business curriculum and separate specialized courses devoted solely to the development of business communication skills. Widespread implementation of these components will surely be helpful in facilitating communication for business.

ACCEPTING SPECIAL RESPONSIBILITIES

Business educators who specialize in the business communication area must also accept additional responsibilities. They must conduct the types of research and other scholarly activities that are needed to advance the discipline of business communication. They must train prospective and practicing business educators to teach business communication content effectively. In addition, they must provide training programs that meet the communication skill needs of business employees and offer consultative services that help businesses resolve their communication-related problems.

Conducting research and other scholarly activities. Business educators who specialize in business communication need to conduct the types of research and other scholarly activities that strengthen the discipline. Chief among the issues that need to be resolved is what the nature of business communication is. A lack of consensus among those with backgrounds in such contributing fields as business education, communication, English, and speech is at least partially responsible for the unclear, inconsistent focus for business communication instruction at various educational levels. When general agreement about the nature of business communication exists among its interdisciplinary practitioners, a more unified effort can be made that advances communication skills for business.

Other major issues that ought to be addressed through research and scholarly thought include (1) prerequisite skills for enrollment in business communication courses at various instructional levels, (2) course content at various instructional levels and relationships to other courses, other departments, and business needs, (3) effective methods for teaching business communication by infusion and by separate courses at various instructional levels, (4) competency levels and evaluation and grading standards at various instructional levels, and (5) qualifications of business communication teachers.

Training teachers. Specialists in the teaching of business communication must train prospective and practicing business educators to teach business communication content effectively. Using their broad knowledge, skill, and attitude bases about various aspects of business communication, they should determine meaningful instructional goals and objectives for those who will teach communication skills for business. Then they ought to determine the most effective ways of preparing others to teach communication skills for business and secure appropriate instructional resources so that the established goals and objectives can be attained. Next they should train others how to teach through a judicious mixture of theoretical and applied activities. Intent on improving their training programs for teachers, they ought to solicit constructive criticism of their efforts and refine their instructional programs. Inasmuch as is feasible, they should monitor the success of their trainees in teaching communication skills for business and offer whatever assistance is appropriate when problems arise.

Training employees. Business educators specializing in business communication must also accept responsibility for providing training programs that meet the needs of business employees when they are asked to do so.

162

Once the business decision is made that employees need additional communication skill training, they should determine the goals and objectives of training programs in consultation with the business executives who oversee the employee training function. Business communication specialists then ought to identify the best methods for achieving the training goals and objectives. Relevant instructional resources that are already prepared should be gathered, and needed new ones should be created. When sufficient instructional resources are available so that the training goals and objectives can be achieved, business communication specialists should either conduct the training programs or select and possibly prepare other qualified individuals to train the business employees. At the end of the training program or at a later date, the effectiveness of the training program ought to be measured, and the results should be reported to the business executives in charge of employee training.

Offering consultative services. Business communication specialists, drawing upon personal expertise and that of others, should also offer consultative services that help businesses resolve their communication-related problems. They should be ready, willing, and able to address usual and unusual communication-based concerns that business executives perceive as detrimental to efficient business operations. Business communication specialists should accept responsibility for addressing and resolving every kind of communication problem by responding to requests from businesspersons for assistance.

Those who specialize in the business communication area must accept several additional responsibilities. They must conduct relevant research and other forms of scholarly activity that keep the discipline vital, train others to teach business communication content effectively, provide training programs for employees of businesses, and offer consultative services that resolve the communication-related problems of businesses. When these specialized responsibilities plus the basic responsibilities are accepted and fulfilled, the phrase *facilitating communication for business* will aptly characterize the efforts of business educators.

CONCLUSION

Facilitating communication for business must be a major goal for all business educators. To accomplish this essential goal and better meet the needs of the business community, all business educators must understand the foundations of business communication, develop specializations that strengthen communication skill instruction, and teach relevant business communication skills in every assigned course. Furthermore, those who specialize in the business communication area must conduct needed research and other scholarly activities, train others to teach business communication content effectively, provide training programs for employees of businesses, and offer consultative services to help businesses resolve their communication-related problems. When business educators as a group accept and fulfill their responsibilities for communication skill development, they will earn the respect of businesspersons for facilitating communication for business.